HJ

D0309469

SM

# LETTERS TO GEORGE

## The account of a rehearsal

*George Farquhar*
*1677-1707*

# Max Stafford-Clark

# LETTERS TO GEORGE

## The account of a rehearsal

N
H
B

NICK HERN BOOKS
A division of Walker Books Limited

*Letters to George* first published in 1989 by Nick Hern Books,
a division of Walker Books Limited,
87 Vauxhall Walk, London SE11 5HJ

British Library Cataloguing in Publication Data
Stafford-Clark, Max
  Letters to George: the account of a
  rehearsal.
  1. Great Britain. Theatre. Production—
  Personal Observations
  I. Title
  792'.0232'0924

ISBN 1-85459-080-4

Typeset by Book Ens, Saffron Walden, Essex
Printed and bound by Billings of Worcester

*To Ann*

# LIST OF ILLUSTRATIONS

# ACKNOWLEDGEMENTS

I hope that, in this account of a rehearsal period, I have emphasised the collaborative nature of theatre. Certainly it's a pleasure to begin by acknowledging the great debt I owe to the Company I worked with last summer. It was a happy occasion. The actors in *The Recruiting Officer* and *Our Country's Good* were Jude Akuwudike, Linda Bassett, Jim Broadbent, Ron Cook, Nick Dunning, Alphonsia Emmanuel, David Haig, Mark Lambert, Lesley Sharp and Mossie Smith. Philip Howard was my good-tempered and loyal Assistant Director, and the stage-management team was led by Neil O'Malley. To them and to all my staff at the Royal Court I owe a debt that it is a pleasure to acknowledge. Some of them are mentioned in these letters; all of them are responsible for the high standard of work we were able to attain.

Vivien Bellamy is the Curator of the Shrewsbury Museum Service and she gave us a wonderful and instructive day in Shrewsbury. I must also thank Nigel Gaspar, Dr Dudley Ireland and Geoffrey Parfitt, who maintained the high standards of Salopian hospitality noted by George Farquhar. John Haynes took the photographs of our trip in Shrewsbury and was my companion on the riverside walks. He is also responsible for the fine photographs of the production. Ron Cook's photos revealed that if he ever wants to give up his day job an alternative profession beckons. Alan McCormack was the director of the compelling production *The Love of a Good Man* at her Majesty's Wormwood Scrubs. Most of the actors are still guests of Her Majesty. I wish she knew what talent she had at her disposal.

My debt to Professor Robert Hume is recorded in the letters themselves, but Jim Fowler and Rhiannon Finamore at the excellent Theatre Museum were incredibly helpful and patient with me at a later stage. They were trusty guides in what was to me the untracked jungle of eighteenth-century theatre history.

Without them, my sketchy knowledge would have remained incomplete.

Ann Pennington listened to me reading her bits of script at most times of the day or night with reasonable patience. She gave me equal measures of encouragement and stern exhortation. If any crass moments remain it is certainly not down to her. Mel Kenyon typed the script and was the first person to read the whole book. I owe heartfelt thanks to her timely enthusiasm.

Finally, I had the privilege of working with three fine authors, all of whom have contributed to this book more than they are aware: George Farquhar, Thomas Keneally and Timberlake Wertenbaker.

Max Stafford-Clark
May 1989

Cast and Crew of the Royal Court Theatre
production of

# THE RECRUITING OFFICER

by George Farquhar


Mr Balance ⎱ *Two Justices* ................. Mark Lambert
Mr Scruple ⎰ ............... Jude Akuwudike
**Mr Worthy**, *a gentleman of Shropshire* ......... Nick Dunning
**Captain Plume**, *a recruiting officer* .............. David Haig
**Captain Brazen**, *a recruiting officer* .............. Ron Cook
**Kite**, *Sergeant to Plume* .................... Jim Broadbent
**Bullock**, *a country clown* ..................... Ron Cook
**Costar Pearmain**, *a recruit* ................. Jude Akuwudike
**Thomas Appletree**, *a recruit* ................. Linda Bassett
**Pluck**, *a butcher* ........................ Mark Lambert
**Bridewell**, *a constable* .................... Nick Dunning
**Servant** *to Justice Balance* ................... Jude Akuwudike
**Melinda**, *a lady of fortune* ................... Linda Bassett
**Silvia**, *daughter to Balance, in love with PLUME* ... Lesley Sharp
**Lucy**, *Melinda's maid* ................ Alphonsia Emmanuel
**Rose**, *a country wench* ..................... Mossie Smith

ALL OTHER PARTS PLAYED BY MEMBERS OF THE COMPANY

Directed by.......................... Max Stafford-Clark
Designed by ........................... Peter Hartwell
Lighting by......................... Christopher Toulmin
Costume Supervisor ...................... Marion Weise
Assistant Director ....................... Philip Howard
Stage Manager .......................... Neil O'Malley
Deputy Stage Manager ................... Nicole Griffiths
Assistant Stage Manager ................. Mark Ormerod

The play takes place in Shrewsbury in the late summer of 1704
following the Battle of Blenheim in August of that year.

Cast and Crew of the Royal Court Theatre
production of

## OUR COUNTRY'S GOOD

by Timberlake Wertenbaker
based on Thomas Keneally's novel THE PLAYMAKER

**Captain Arthur Phillip, RN,**
  *Governor General of New South Wales* . . . . . . . . . . . Ron Cook
**Major Robbie Ross, RM** . . . . . . . . . . . . . . . . . Mark Lambert
**Captain David Collins, RM,** *Advocate General* . Nick Dunning
**Captain Watkin Tench, RM** . . . . . . . . . . . . . . Jude Akuwudike
**Captain Jemmy Campbell, RM** . . . . . . . . . . . . Jim Broadbent
**Reverend Johnson** . . . . . . . . . . . . . . . . . . . . . . . . Lesley Sharp
**Lieutenant George Johnston, RM** . . . . Alphonsia Emmanuel
**Lieutenant Will Dawes, RM** . . . . . . . . . . . . . . Linda Bassett
**2nd Lieutenant Ralph Clark, RM** . . . . . . . . . . . . . David Haig
**2nd Lieutenant William Faddy, RM** . . . . . . . . . Mossie Smith
**Midshipman Harry Brewer, RN,**
  *Provost Marshal* . . . . . . . . . . . . . . . . . . . . . . . . Jim Broadbent
**An Aboriginal Australian** . . . . . . . . . . . . . . . . Jude Akuwudike
**John Arscott** . . . . . . . . . . . . . . . . . . . . . . . . . . . Jim Broadbent
**Thomas Barrett** . . . . . . . . . . . . . . . . . . . . . . . Jude Akuwudike
**Black Caesar** . . . . . . . . . . . . . . . . . . . . . . . . . Jude Akuwudike
**Ketch Freeman** . . . . . . . . . . . . . . . . . . . . . . . . . Mark Lambert
**Robert Sideway** . . . . . . . . . . . . . . . . . . . . . . . . . Nick Dunning
**John Wisehammer** . . . . . . . . . . . . . . . . . . . . . . . . . Ron Cook
**Mary Brenham** . . . . . . . . . . . . . . . . . . . . . . . . . . Lesley Sharp
**Dabby Bryant** . . . . . . . . . . . . . . . . . . . . . . . . . . Mossie Smith
**Liz Morden** . . . . . . . . . . . . . . . . . . . . . . . . . . . . Linda Bassett
**Duckling Smith** . . . . . . . . . . . . . . . . . Alphonsia Emmanuel
**Meg Long** . . . . . . . . . . . . . . . . . . . . . . . . . . . . . . Lesley Sharp

Directed by . . . . . . . . . . . . . . . . . . . . . . . . . . Max Stafford-Clark
Designed by . . . . . . . . . . . . . . . . . . . . . . . . . . . . Peter Hartwell
Lighting by . . . . . . . . . . . . . . . . . . . . . . . . . . . . . . . Jenny Cane
Sound by . . . . . . . . . . . . . . . . . . . . . . . . . . . . . . . Bryan Bowen
Costume Supervisor . . . . . . . . . . . . . . . . . . . . . . Marion Weise
Assistant Director . . . . . . . . . . . . . . . . . . . . . . . Philip Howard
Stage Manager . . . . . . . . . . . . . . . . . . . . . . . . . Neil O'Malley
Deputy Stage Manager . . . . . . . . . . . . . . . . . . Mark Ormerod
Assistant Stage Manager . . . . . . . . . . . . . . . . . Nicole Griffiths

The play takes place in Sydney, Australia in 1789

# INTRODUCTION

New York usually works a heady excitement of its own. But, in January 1988, I was becoming fretful. There seemed a lot of waiting around. No matter how grave or pertinent the subject of any play performed in New York it immediately becomes subsumed by the much graver question of whether or not it is a huge hit. To run or not to run, is the only question. It was while waiting to learn the Manhattan currency valuation on *Serious Money* that I began writing to George Farquhar. I was staying at the Algonquin Hotel, which would give anyone the feeling they ought to write, and my duties were light. *Serious Money* had been previewing for weeks and the actors were excellent, although exhausted from struggling nightly with a wilful Broadway audience who really wanted the play to be rather less incisive in its critique of capitalism. I already knew that my next project was to be the linked productions of *The Recruiting Officer* and *Our Country's Good*, but I needed someone to talk to to make it tangible so I wrote to George.

A few weeks later, back in London, I was absorbed in running the Royal Court, applying for my own job and in directing *Bloody Poetry* by Howard Brenton. I couldn't write. And even when I began casting and planning both productions I was a desultory correspondent. During the workshop for *Our Country's Good* I was involved in new relationships with Timberlake and the actors, and it was only when we began rehearsal for *The Recruiting Officer* in June that I needed George every day. I realised that it was the first time in over fifteen years I had been in rehearsal without a writer. I don't always get on well with playwrights. Their obsessions are the banner we directors fight under and this doesn't always make for an easy relationship. But I missed George terribly. In rehearsal all of us began to consult him on a fairly regular basis. 'What does George mean here?' or 'How serious is George about this?' Occasionally, one of the actors would take on

George's voice and talk back. Lesley Sharp and Nick Dunning sounded particularly authentic. I imagined Farquhar looking and speaking like the actor Adrian Dunbar in his role in *The Pope's Wedding*. Adrian would then have been 28, the same age George was when he wrote *The Recruiting Officer*. Adrian is from Enniskillen whereas George was from Derry, but I imagined both to have the same fresh-cheeked, country-boy enthusiasm, the same sharp wit and curiosity about the theatre and about London.

I dropped into the habit of writing to George every night when I got home. They were often just notes about what had happened in rehearsal that day and about what I hoped to get done tomorrow. But I came to depend on a nightly exchange of views with George. I've tried not to alter these letters much, although I have eliminated some of the repetition and some of the more fearful banalities. Looking at them now, some of them seem gloomy and pessimistic but then I was entrusting George with my insecurities. Once we began rehearsal for *Our Country's Good* in August, I lapsed back into merely occasional correspondence as I shifted loyalties to Timberlake.

I had always known somewhere in the back of my mind that there had been a convict production of *The Recruiting Officer* in the early days of the Australian penal colony, and I read Thomas Keneally's thrilling novel sometime in the autumn of 1987. *The Playmaker* is an imaginative reconstruction of the events surrounding the rehearsal of this production for the King's birthday on 4 June 1789. At the same time, I was engaged on the Royal Court's bi-annual search for a classic. From time to time it's important for a theatre primarily engaged in producing new writing on a public stage to measure its standards against the past. In its early days, the English Stage Company at the Royal Court had produced a high proportion of classics. Perhaps William Gaskill's 1968 production of *Macbeth* with Alec Guinness and Simone Signoret stands out. And in my own time there had been Richard Eyre's memorable production of *Hamlet* with Jonathan Pryce. I had directed *The Seagull* in an Irish adaptation by Thomas Kilroy in 1981, and in 1986 I had commissioned Howard Barker to re-edit the first four acts of Thomas Middleton's *Women Beware Women* and, in a second half, to write his own conclusion. These had all been fairly active attempts at messing about with the classics. They had all begun with a strong idea of how to re-approach a major play. A Restoration play seemed a possibility for 1988 since the casting requirements weren't as enormous as Shakespeare or the Jacobean writers. And I had been much taken with Peter James's production of *The Beaux' Stratagem* at the Lyric, Hammersmith, in 1984. The directness in that play of Farquhar's attack on marriage and the deadly picture of Squire Sullen and Mrs Sullen were vivid and original.

Halfway through reading *The Playmaker* I began re-reading *The Recruiting Officer* and the idea took hold both of reviving *The Recruiting Officer* and of commissioning an adaptation of Thomas Keneally's novel. Like all my predecessors at the Royal Court, I longed for a more permanent acting ensemble and part of the appeal was that the two halves of the joint project were very different. To revive a major classic unseen in London for over twenty years and to collaborate with a writer in making an adaptation of Keneally's novel would draw on very different skills both from me and from the acting company. The responsibility of a director reviving a classic is to make it live firstly for the actors and secondly for the audience by uncovering and living through the moral imperatives that are the sinews of the play. Sometimes, you approach this task by researching and reading about the period, and on other occasions you jolt the audience into a new awareness by relocating the play in a different era or setting. I had done this with the Thomas Kilroy version of *The Seagull*, setting it in the County Galway of rent strikes and the Celtic Movement. The job of collaborating with a contemporary writer to turn an idea into a play is much harder to define . . . and yet perversely enough I had much more experience of this way of working.

Work with the Joint Stock Theatre Group in the seventies had on several occasions taken a book as its starting point, for instance, *The Speakers* or *Fanshen*. The starting point was a three- or four-week workshop with the actors and the writer, in which the themes of the book were researched and explored by the whole group. But although we intruded dangerously into the writer's creative process, Joint Stock's success was in knowing when to stop. The four-week workshop was followed by a nine- or ten-week gap during which the writer wrote the play, free to draw on whatever aspect of the research they chose. Towards the end of this period the first draft would emerge, and the dialogue with the rest of the company would begin again. During the more conventional rehearsal period that followed, the play would often go through several drafts before emerging in its final form. It's a hazardous and demanding way of working. Hazardous for the writers because they have to surrender a certain degree of autonomy and because their work is constantly open to question and examination. For the actors, it's alarming because they commit to the workshop and endure the unpaid gap without ever knowing what part they will play, how large it will be and how rewarding. And for the director it is nerve-racking because there is no script; no map of the journey he is making. But it is also thrilling. The commitment of the whole group is powerful, and there is a heady excitement as the actors discover previously untapped researching and interviewing skills. For the writer it's an opportunity to get out of the garret; and the focus on meeting people and on the sheer unexpectedness of real life seems to lead to a closer encounter with truth than the theatre often provides. The decision to make a play in this way necessitates better working conditions too. From the puny Royal Court budget we chiselled out eight weeks of rehearsal, including the workshop for *Our Country's Good* and another five weeks for rehearsing *The Recruiting Officer*. In this time, you can achieve a depth and detail to the work that is just not feasible in a conventional four-week rehearsal period. The inability of drama critics to perceive the basic relationship between economic firepower and the quality of the work is the one thing that never fails to make me incandescent with rage. Peter Brook and Peter Stein are very fine directors, but what I envy is not their talent but their ability to organize lengthy rehearsal periods. Talent plus funding equals genius.

I talked to Timberlake Wertenbaker about writing a play based on Tom Keneally's novel early in January 1988. I knew her socially. She had attended the weekly Script Meetings at the Royal Court, and during my tenure she had had two plays produced, *Abel's Sister* in the Theatre Upstairs and *The Grace of Mary Traverse* on the Main Stage in October 1985. Set in the mid-eighteenth century this latter was the striking tale of a well-connected girl who plunges onwards in a journey of self-discovery but finds that only men are allowed to discover the world. The play ends with the Gordon Riots. I found the play intelligent, theatrical and perceptive, and I had commissioned a further piece from her. I was delighted when she was interested in the Australian project. We agreed on a schedule. We would do a brief two-week workshop at the end of April. We would officially begin rehearsal on 6 June for seven weeks. The first two weeks would also be mainly devoted to the Australian project, before the actors began rehearsing *The Recruiting Officer*, whose first preview was set for 20 July. At this point the actors would begin rehearsal for Timberlake's play and would stay on a schedule giving four performances a week of *The Recruiting Officer* until we opened the new play on 1 September. This wasn't ideal, but it was an attempt to give us the longest possible rehearsal time while still earning some money from the box office without totally exhausting the actors. It was a workable compromise. And it nearly worked.

In any new play, the relationship between the writer and director is crucial. In a project of this kind it becomes closer than a marriage. It's like a two-handed trans-Atlantic voyage in an open boat. I had worked several times with Caryl Churchill in this way, and we had evolved a close understanding, but it was some years since I had attempted the same relationship with anybody else. Timberlake is a striking woman of great elegance and wit. She has a style and chic that her name and her Basque/Canadian background would suggest. The two-week workshop was a honeymoon as we uncovered the extraordinary facts of transportation, incarceration and the First Fleet's encounter with Australia. Later in August, when rehearsals started, we drew the bile from each other's personalities. She defended her script with pugnacious and inflexible stubbornness while I sometimes exposed its shortcomings with malice and a certain cruelty. But, even in those dog days, she would arrive at the Royal Court at noon in her battered Renault, exhausted and drained, having spent the morning writing, park on a zig-zag line, summon Philip Howard, the assistant director, drop the keys in his hand and bid him park the car. I was always impressed by the elan and confidence of this gesture. Confidence was what we needed at that point. With her copper-coloured hair she looked rather like one of the portraits of Queen Elisabeth, but Philip called her 'The Baroness' and the name stuck.

Reading back over my correspondence with George, I realise that it reveals as much about my growing curiosity about eighteenth-century theatre as it does about my own rehearsal methods. It's certainly a partial and partisan account of rehearsal that is far from comprehensive. But then I didn't set out to write a day-by-day guide to directing technique. I love directing and I sometimes enjoy teaching, but I'm wary of observers who crave a day or a week in rehearsal to sit at the feet and learn. I admire their enthusiasm but I'm suspicious of the mystification of the process. You wouldn't learn much about farming by following a farmer for a day. It's a year round job. It's the same with directing. I'm not aware of having evolved any particular philosophy. I really believe in the pragmatic solution of specific problems by any method that works. All I can say is that my methods work some of the time. Through rehearsal I enjoyed learning more about the methods George might have employed. The letters also wander into territory that is really more occupied by *Our Country's Good* but I make no apology for that. Our increasing understanding of George's theatre, for instance, helped realise some scenes in *Our Country's Good*, just as Ralph Clark's details of wardroom life on HMS Friendship helped me comprehend aspects of Captain Plume's relationship with Sergeant Kite. At this distance, the two rehearsals have become fused in my mind, a state of affairs which is aptly reflected in these letters.

Max Stafford-Clark

# Monday, 18 January 1988

## Dear George Farquhar,

I hope you will pardon my writing to you so abruptly, but I'm going to be directing a production of *The Recruiting Officer* at the Royal Court Theatre this summer and it seems important to contact you somehow or other. Hence these letters. The plan is to have a company of actors who will appear in both your play and an adaptation of Thomas Keneally's novel *The Playmaker*. Keneally's novel concerns events surrounding the production of your play in 1789 in the Australian penal colony. It was the first play to be performed on the Australian continent. The convict who plays Melinda is charged with stealing food from the colony's stores and the young Marine Lieutenant, who is the director of the play, falls in love with Mary Brenham, the convict playing Silvia. The Governor General of the penal colony is a liberal and supports the production, while the Senior Marine Officer is fervently opposed to the principle of convict recreation. The production goes ahead. The power of the play is triumphant.

One thing that strikes me about the story is that it catches people at a moment when there's a possibility of change. Performing the play becomes, for Keneally's convicts, a way of re-establishing a relationship with humanity and civilization. A lot of work I've directed has concerned itself with people at a similar point. In *Light Shining in Buckinghamshire*, Caryl Churchill focused on a disparate group of country people in the years after Cromwell's overthrow of Charles I. For them, religion is the key that unlocks the possibility of change. David Hare's *Fanshen*, adapted from William Hinton's book, was about the effort of one village in China to put into practice the principles of communism that had utterly transformed the villagers' lives.

It will be thrilling to rehearse your great comedy, and then work on an adaptation of Keneally's novel. The actors will be seen rehearsing the same parts in the adaptation as they will play in *The Recruiting Officer*. This will involve a certain

1

amount of doubling up as we will only be able to afford a company of nine or, at the most, ten actors.

I should make it clear that, although I am a director of some experience, I've worked on very few classics. This will be the first play in over ten years that I will direct without the writer in rehearsal. You will be much missed, so I'm eager to keep in touch from time to time. I'm in New York at the moment, waiting for *Serious Money* to open on Broadway. They believe in endless previews here to test the product, as once the critics are unleashed that's often the end of it. There have been twenty previews already. I understand that in your day three nights in succession was considered a long run. I don't think you would have enjoyed Broadway very much, although you would have had a very good time at the Algonquin Hotel, where they treat writers with great respect.

# Tuesday, 26 January 1988

## Dear George Farquhar,

I'm back at the Royal Court now and it occurs to me that you may find the term 'director' confusing. The responsibilities involved would, in your day, have been divided between the prompter, the author and a senior actor. I should have realized that the word is relatively modern. I believe that Tom Robertson, in the middle of the last century, was the first person to undertake responsibility for co-ordinating every aspect of a production and imposing an overall vision on the whole production. And I think the term 'director' or 'producer' was first used then. In recent years, this has often led to directors having overall responsibility for the finances, programming and running of a theatre, and, in this aspect of their jobs, they would be familiar to you as 'theatre managers'. There's no doubt that, over the last hundred years, most of the radical innovations in theatre have been led by directors: Stanislavsky, Brecht, Meyerhold, Reinhardt, Peter Brook, Joan Littlewood. Yet, at present, the term is discredited. Actors think directors have too much control. Any group of actors in their first tea-break delight each other with horror stories of directorial incompetence, and it is true that it is much easier for a director of modest ability to achieve security and power than it is even for an outstanding leading actor. But the fact that some poor directors flourish shouldn't obscure the vital importance of the job today. I understand the impatience expressed by actors, but I don't see how the centrality of the role can be diminished without harming the theatre as a whole.

My own ideals of theatre were formed in the now discredited Sixties and my passions were fired by a number of lively American companies: The Living Theatre, The Open Theatre, and The La Mama Troupe, who expressed an idea of total theatre that I thought exhilarating. The spirit of the ensemble seemed pre-eminent and I was somehow able to overlook the fact that these companies were autocratically led by some strong-minded and

3

determined directors: the Becks, Joseph Chaikin and Tom O'Horgan. But the idea of collaboration took hold and on the few occasions when I have been able to work with a more permanent ensemble of actors and when, either by accident or by design, there has been a genuine effort to share power and responsibility, it has created the best working conditions I've known. And this in turn has led to the best work. Theatre is a collaborative act and, when the conditions for true collaboration can be created, theatre hits its most thrilling potential. Everybody in theatre really knows this but, because it is so difficult to achieve and so impossible to sustain, we all manage to evade it. This means directors end up directing classics, where they don't have to deal with the difficult relationship with the writer; the writers wish to direct their own plays, so they're not challenged by a director's imagination; and actors wish to start their own companies, which is a fashionable idea but in practice the work often becomes vapid and facile.

I'm concerned about the number of actors we will able to afford. But economic factors must have played some part in your theatre too. It's noticeable that, while Shakespeare or Webster wrote for a company of eighteen or so, your plays and those of other writers we casually lump together as 'Restoration dramatists' could be done with a cast of fourteen or fifteen. *The Recruiting Officer* has nine men, who appear in more than one scene and another four women's parts but, in addition, there are numerous footmen, poachers, justices, constables and the generically named 'mob'. The conclusion I draw is that the plays centred on fewer principal actors but that there was no restraint on having as many smaller character roles as you wished. The smaller cast gives a different feeling. Restoration plays are less epic, rather more domestic in tone, and must be the first plays to have been set in England at the time they were written. Shakespeare sets his plays in Denmark or Italy or Cyprus or Ancient Britain, and the action took place in a variety of periods other than at the time that he was writing. I'm unclear how the doubling can work for *The Recruiting Officer* but I will be in touch again as soon as I have some actors in mind.

I am rather alarmed by the news that the National Theatre and Royal Shakespeare Company are also planning productions of *The Recruiting Officer*. Of course, it's possible that the different approaches will lead to a fascinating re-appraisal of your work but I think all of us would worry about the box

4

office repercussions. I fear the RSC's plans are already well developed for a production that Barry Kyle will direct.

Bill Alexander from the RSC left me various messages last week; perhaps this is what it is about. I'll call him back as soon as possible. I did know that Declan Donnellan was considering *The Recruiting Officer* as one of several plays he may undertake at the National, but I don't think this has got so far.

I understand that the popularity of *The Recruiting Officer* has led to simultaneous productions before – there were productions both at Drury Lane and at the Haymarket on the same night within six months of the first performance, in 1710. Because a writer received the box office receipts from the third performance only, it seems a long run didn't necessarily lead to wealth. Nowadays, a successful run on Broadway can make a playwright very wealthy indeed, but it's impossible for *The Recruiting Officer* to follow *Serious Money* on that particular route. There are seventeen dark theatres, nine musicals and three straight plays on Broadway at the moment and *Serious Money* is only there because of the topicality of the subject. I don't think it will stay long.* The subject of money has got a lot more serious since the Wall Street Crash of last October 19th.

*It didn't.

5

# Sunday, January 31st

## Dear George Farquhar,

I had a meeting with Bill Alexander last Thursday. I hoped he was going to offer me a job, but although he was very charming, he stopped some way short of this point. He explained the difficulties of running the Barbican and what a grave responsibility it was. He explained how well *The Recruiting Officer* would suit his company . . . how excellent a Sergeant Kite Brian Cox would make, and how superb a Melinda Fiona Shaw would be, and he finally asked rather anxiously in what period I intended to set your play. Good Dame Gossip (a.k.a. Brian Cox) had already told me that the director, Barry Kyle, intended to relocate *The Recruiting Officer* in the First World War. I knew this and was tempted to tell Bill that I had thought of setting it in 1916. However, I thought that would be stirring it up too much. We agreed to co-operate as much as possible, market a joint playtext, do some joint publicity and so forth. (God knows what that means, since we have a publicity budget that won't even permit us to run ads in the classifieds these days.) He told me the RSC production would open in October and I told Bill ours would be in repertoire with the Keneally adaptation by the beginning of September. This wasn't really a lie, but I left myself a bit of room. The bastards! They're already doing *The Constant Couple* this summer and a tour of *The Beaux' Strategem* in the autumn; they should re-christen themselves the RFC or, given their latest sponsorship deal, The Royal Insurance/Royal Farquhar Company. Because, make no mistake about it, we're anybody's these days, George. For a couple of thousand quid, we would become the Cadbury's Drinking Chocolate Royal Court. At least your sponsors gave rather classier names: The Lord Admiral's Men or The Duke of Exeter's Men.

I think setting *The Recruiting Officer* in the First World War will have its problems. Kite's recruiting methods would seem a bit superfluous in a war which saw the largest number of volunteers in history. Nice frocks though.

Bill said to remember how small your world was . . . just a few people doing plays in two theatres in London for rather a small and enclosed audience. Not the confidence of Shakespeare's period. Theatres could be closed . . . the Puritans had shown that. The 1706 *Spotlight* (the actor's directory) must have been a thin volume. There couldn't have been more than thirty actors and a dozen actresses who earned a living from the stage in London.

# Tuesday, February 9th

*Dear George Farquhar,*

Perhaps you would prefer a production at the National Theatre which would refocus major attention on your work. But loyalty is a particular characteristic ascribed to you by friends and biographers alike, so perhaps you'd be swayed in my favour by our both having spent time at Trinity College, Dublin. I should also point out that, like you, I was brought up a Protestant, although I can't say it has been a dominant influence. As for my rivals, I'm afraid I can't shed any light on Barry Kyle's religious beliefs, nor can I reassure you in any way about Declan Donnellan, although he comes from Roscommon and the name certainly sounds suspicious.

I understand that lack of money meant you had to wait on tables for other undergraduates during your time at Trinity, which must have been dispiriting. And that you left to join the theatre without graduating. So did I. Dublin is now, as then, a great city for the drama. It may surprise you to learn that you are reckoned to be the second, after your contemporary at Trinity, William Congreve. in a great line of Protestant Anglo-Irish dramatists. Outside the front gate of the college there's a statue of Oliver Goldsmith. R.B. Sheridan, Oscar Wilde and Samuel Beckett were also Trinity students. If you also add those other two great Irish Protestant writers, Bernard Shaw and Sean O'Casey, then there is an extraordinary line-up. I don't know why this should be. Some say it's because of the importance that has always been accorded to debate in Ireland. This may be so: the other great Irish gift is for oratory, and from Grattan and Burke (whose statues – permanently in mid-sentence – address the façade of Trinity as well) to Bernadette Devlin, Irish speakers have been among the most charismatic in the House of Commons. Myself, I think it's something to do with the size and humanity of one of Europe's smallest capitals, and the importance of cultural achievement in an Anglo-Irish society that had daily to maintain its elevated position. It was also one way of impressing the English. And it's notable that, although most of Ireland's playwrights received their education and training in Dublin, their reputations were made on the stages of London. The Protestant work ethic must also be a motivating factor. It's certainly acknowledged by Ingmar Bergman, one of the great writers and directors of our time, who, like you, is the son of a Protestant minister.

Also, there's the high status accorded to the writer throughout Irish society. I once spent an evening in a Dublin bar with another great Irish playwright, Brendan Behan. But already this sounds misleading. I was in a bar, the Lincoln Inn off Nassau Street, with a fellow student. Other groups, with Behan in one of them, were drinking as well. In the course of the evening the various groups flowed together and became one. I was very much at the edge of it. Politics were discussed, James Joyce aired, the qualities of different stouts were analysed and debated. Songs were sung. It was a wonderful, harmonious evening. One to remember. Not drunken, not rowdy. Behan was the effortless and charismatic centre of the group and not once was he permitted to pay for a drink. Long live patronage of the Arts, George.

# Saturday, February 20th

## Dear George,

I very much enjoy the lull between productions. I'm poised now between the different productions of *Serious Money* and a period of intense work that will begin in two weeks with Howard Brenton's *Bloody Poetry* and end with the opening of *Our Country's Good* in September. I went to the theatre twice today. In the afternoon, I saw the matinée of *A View from the Bridge*, by Arthur Miller, at the Aldwych and, in the evening, I saw the last performance of the Goldoni plays, *Countrymania*, directed by Mike Alfreds, in the Olivier. The first was packed and the audience thrilled to Michael Gambon's mighty performance. I think he's a fine actor but I could see the simple emotional shorthand he had to embrace in order to unify the excited house. On the other hand, the Goldoni plays pleased nobody. The actors were a hand-picked company of our youngest and finest; Mike Alfreds is one of the directors in this country whose work I really esteem, and yet the few hundred people spread round the rim of the Olivier were denied any theatrical occasion. I think beyond a certain size theatre demands stars or spectacle. The detail of company work, which interests both Mike Alfreds and me, becomes diffused. The fineness of his work, which I so much admired in his Marivaux productions at the Lyric Studio, was lost.

By coincidence, *Serious Money* closes on Broadway tonight and I think the same lesson applies. At the Royal Court (seating 395), Caryl Churchill's play was an electrifying experience; when it transferred to Wyndham's (seating 780), it was hard work to communicate the complexity and fascination of the financial world, and the actors reckoned they were able to pull it off only one night in three; on Broadway, at the Royale (seating 1,200), it was an impossible and disheartening job.

Drafting Kate Nelligan into the company was an acknowledgement that the event had insufficient pulling power. It's the same with rock stars. I remember seeing Bruce Springsteen support a guy called Biff Rose at Max's, Kansas City. I thought he was terrific. I wouldn't pay the tube fare to see him at Wembley, where the best view would be on a giant projection screen.

How many people did *The Recruiting Officer* play to at its first performance? I must find out. I don't think it could have been more than about five hundred.

Certainly the inverse works. I once did a production in Edinburgh, at the Traverse Theatre, that played to an audience of just one person per night. The show was called *U2*. Very sixties. Very Traverse Workshop Company. Anybody who rang to book for the show was told it was sold out but to leave their name on a waiting list. From this list we selected one person at random . . . As they arrived in the theatre the lights went down. An exotically dressed dancer, Linda Goddard, appeared to float towards them while they were thus disorientated; in fact, she was on a swing. After dancing for the solitary audience, she led them down the fire escape and through the alleys and wynds of the Old Town, where various scenes of marital discord were re-enacted. Arriving at the Old Traverse, which now served as accommodation for the Traverse Workshop Company, the spectator was induced to sit in a darkened room. Further scenes of disintegrating relationships were acted next door and the spectator was invited to watch through a keyhole. It embarrasses me to relate more but I think that finally, to sitar music, the person's feet were washed in a bowl and then dried by a woman's hair. This was Annie Russell, who had hair down to her waist. The purpose of the experiment was to discover what authority and control an acting company had over an audience when the ratio of actors to audience was pushed to its most extreme.

The results were startling: our power was total. We only did eight performances but we could have got those eight people to do anything. Our American drama professor wished to resign his tenure to join the company.

So, I'm certainly not a populist, George. In fact, I'm an exclusivist. I prefer the power granted to the actors by a relatively intimate auditorium. This isn't a view that would be supported by writers like David Edgar or Trevor Griffiths, who see the danger of smaller theatres becoming ghettoes for radical work. And Howard Brenton's famous phrase, 'I long to get my hands on a Steinway', showed his determination to get to the National's larger stages. I don't share his enthusiasm. I think *Countrymania* would have been a vivid experience in a smaller

11

house, and I resent the insistent focus on one personality, and the coarsening of technique, that larger theatres demand.

# Thursday, March 17th

*Dear George,*

           I'm sorry I haven't been in touch but I've started rehearsals for Howard Brenton's *Bloody Poetry* and I haven't had much time. Also, my mind hasn't been on *The Recruiting Officer* very much, although I must talk to you about actors soon. I think Nigel Terry is going to be a wonderful Byron in Howard's play which is, of course, about writing. The relationship between Byron and Shelley is the centre of the play. There's a wonderful scene in a gondola, when Byron is tormenting Shelley for endlessly writing about rebellion but doing nothing about it. Brenton puts lines from Shelley's *Julian and Maddalo* into Byron's mouth:

> Most wretched men
> Are cradled into poetry by wrong,
> They learn in suffering what they teach in song.

Howard believes that Byron/Shelley is saying that injustice and inhumanity are what lead 'most wretched men' to write in the first place. Your responsibility as a writer is to explore men's bestiality and inhumanity. But that if you soak yourself for too long, you become infected and unable to write about anything else. Certainly, there are some contemporary playwrights, like Howard Barker or Edward Bond, who appear to have locked themselves into a self-enclosed world of private imagery, which has sporadic contact with either history or contemporary life. Howard Barker's new play, *The Bite of the Night*, has a Helen of Troy who, in the course of the evening's action, has both arms and both legs hacked off. Yet this limbless trunk leaves me unmoved because it is a metaphor that appears to have little life outside itself. Neither of these two great writers is much good at collaborating with their fellow theatre-workers: Howard delivers the play, but takes little part or interest in rehearsals, despite having two companies at the moment specifically dedi-

13

cated to his work; while Edward is now quite unable to relinquish his steely grip on his own work and wishes to direct all his own plays. Since no management relishes this prospect, they remain unperformed. Neither writer has the gift of collaboration. Unable to learn from colleagues, they have to drive their own vision further and further each time they write. As with Ken Russell, the danger is that genius becomes self-parody.

For the creative lives of playwrights are often brutally short. As short as athletes. Vanbrugh wrote only two plays, as did Congreve and Sheridan. And the shores of Sloane Square are littered with colossi from the past, who have forsworn the theatre even as it has spurned them: John Arden, John Osborne, Arnold Wesker, David Storey, Anne Jellicoe aren't much seen on our stages now. I think, in this sense, theatre is the cruellest medium; because it moves so fast and leaves us all behind.

In this sense, George, you had the fortune to die before you were thirty, and at the very peak of your writing career. Your early success, *The Constant Couple*, is now rarely performed, but both *The Recruiting Officer* and *The Beaux' Stratagem* are acknowledged masterpieces. It's a bitter irony that you died (probably of tuberculosis, then as now the disease of poverty) on the night of the third performance of *The Beaux' Stratagem*, when you would have received the box office receipts. What would you have written about if you had lived? I'm sure you would have gone on writing because, unlike your famous predecessors and contemporaries, you would have needed the income. Perhaps I was hasty in thinking that you wouldn't have cared for Broadway. At any rate, you would never have replied to Molière as Vanbrugh was supposed to have done, when the great Frenchman enquired why he was no longer writing: 'Oh no sir, you are mistaken. I am not a writer. I am a gentleman.'

# Sunday, April 10th

## Dear George,

          *Bloody Poetry* is now previewing, but I've had some time to think about casting, and over the last two weeks Timberlake and I have been talking to actors together with Lisa Makin, the Royal Court's casting director. It's possible for the actors to have a reaction to *The Recruiting Officer* but our descriptions of Timberlake's play are entirely speculative, and we can only give them a vague idea of what role they may be playing. Linda Bassett will be Melinda. She and I worked on *Aunt Dan and Lemon* together, as well as on the many different chapters of *Serious Money*. I first worked with David Haig (Captain Plume) and Ron Cook (Captain Brazen) in Andrea Dunbar's *The Arbor*, and I've directed both of them on several occasions since. I have long admired Mossie Smith (Rose) and Lesley Sharp (Silvia) from a distance, although I've never worked with either of them. They were both in Simon Curtis's thrilling production of *Road* by Jim Cartwright. Timberlake knows Nick Dunning (Worthy) from the work they have done together for Shared Experience, and Simon Curtis prompted us to choose Mark Lambert (Justice Balance) who was at the Court in Anne Devlin's *Ourselves Alone*. I don't know Alphonsia Emmanuel (Lucy) at all, although I saw her work at the RSC a couple of years ago. Jim Broadbent (Sergeant Kite) is one of the country's outstanding actors and will be a terrific Kite. Probably the cast is incomplete, but this is a very good team for the workshop. We will add more people later.

    So I've worked with three of the actors before, and I know another three of them pretty well. I usually work with a combination of familiar talent and new faces. It gives the consolation of permanence with the *frisson* of the unknown. Everybody in the theatre worships the idea of an ensemble but financial restrictions, and the different demands of each new play, have always prevented the Court from seriously considering a permanent company. Also, I think actors enjoy the magpie diversity

15

and range of a working actor's life. Or at any rate the diversity that's been available through the Seventies and the first half of the Eighties. In fact, I carry a semi-permanent ensemble in my head, hoping to draw from them in each production. Most directors do the same. I think it's the best that can be done in this country. On the Continent there's quite a different tradition: rather monastic, where actors spend their lives in one company. This isn't necessarily the same as an ensemble. In fact 'ensemble', together with 'workshop', are two of the most abused words in the theatrical dictionary. An ensemble can only be created over a period of time when there's a collective purpose, and a certain equality both of talent and opportunity. While 'workshop' is a euphemism increasingly misused to describe a play unready for performance. In New York ensembles workshop endlessly and preview interminably: all to disappear at either a call from Hollywood or an indifferent notice in the *New York Times*.

Anyway, George, this ensemble are now poised to begin a workshop in a week's time.

# Wednesday, April 13th

## Dear George,

           *Bloody Poetry* opened last night. Goodish reviews, although I don't think they'll do much for business. Nobody seemed to notice the direction much but then they don't if you do new plays. That's why I'm turning to the classics.

I wanted a word about design. Peter Hartwell, the designer, has given me a book of Rowlandson prints, which present a very clear picture of the lively nature of eighteen-century theatre. There's one called *The Prologue* which shows an actor, tricorn hat in hand and calf extended, with an energetic but respectful demeanour, speaking a prologue directly to the audience. They appear cheerful, colourfully dressed, and perhaps a little rumbustious. Although the actor forms the focus, a certain amount of attention is being paid to a lady with a rather daring dress in one of the boxes. Another member of the acting company has his nose poked through the curtain, perhaps in an attempt to assess the evening's punters. There are four boxes, which are placed directly at each side of the stage . . . eight in all. So the actors could chat or give asides directly to an audience placed almost at their elbows. In fact, there's a record of Peg Woffington, Garrick's leading lady, successfully bringing an action against a gentleman who became too familiar during a performance of *King Lear* and fondled her 'with the utmost indecency'.

Of course the house would have been fully lit with huge candelabra, so the relationship between actors and audience was dangerously close. We need to move back to this a little. So why don't we restore the side boxes at the Royal Court and build our own version of an eighteenth-century playhouse? A significant amount of your play is in asides and an intimate and familiar easy relationship with the audience could be an advantage.

In fact, the Royal Court was originally designed with two

17

such boxes on each side of the stage. The bottom ones have long been turned into downstage entrances and the upper two are lighting positions, but it won't be hard to restore them. What prices should we charge? £4 or £12 per seat?*

I already have it in mind to play the first scene – where Sergeant Kite is recruiting the mob in Shrewsbury Market – either on the steps outside the theatre or in the foyer. So the relationship between stage and audience will be established as close right from the start. Let me know what you think. I'm very enthusiastic.

*Are they the best or the worst seats in the house? In the event the public were suspicious of such proximity.

# Sunday, April 17th

## Dear George,

There are one or two casting problems and before I get too involved with the workshop period for *Our Country's Good* next week it seems right to air them. However we split the parts, I don't think I will have enough men in the Company. So I'm going to ask Linda Bassett to play Costar Pearmain's friend, Thomas Appletree, in the recruiting scene. She's a terrific actress; enormously talented and with wonderful integrity and innocence. I imagine you will be surprised by the casting and that you may prefer Appletree to be played by a man.

On the other hand, the history of your early hit, *The Constant Couple*, might just make you pause a little before condemning the whole idea. After your death Peg Woffington exploited the cross-dressing element of Silvia with such success that the public insisted she should play Sir Harry Wildair in *The Constant Couple*. She played the part to great acclaim and enormous public success. In fact, Sir Harry Wildair became a famous 'breeches' role, played by several generations of actresses. I gather the public enjoyed the opportunity of viewing the actresses' legs: in their full length dresses their legs were well out of sight. The sheer sexiness of the Restoration stage is difficult for us to grasp. After all, your first Silvia, Anne Oldfield, and your first Melinda, Jane Rogers, were only the second generation of actresses on the English stage. Then, as now, the public usually chose to go and see a particular performer rather than a particular play, and the excitement of new stars had much to do with the success of your plays. It was also generally felt that Anne and Jane were 'without affectation' and 'closer to nature' than the previous generation of leading ladies who – because they were the first women on the English stage – had had to learn their profession from scratch. Transvestism had existed in Shakespeare, of course, but Viola and Portia would have been played by boys playing women disguised as men.

Anyway, I think you'd like Linda Bassett. She's also playing Melinda.

Another good reason to cast her as Thomas Appletree is that it will train the audience's expectations. Any subsequent doubling won't seem so shocking. An audience will accept most things as long as the convention of the evening is made clear by the production. In *Serious Money* I cast Lesley Manville and Meera Syal as the two stockbrokers in the first scene. I had learnt this lesson with an earlier Joint Stock/Royal Court play. *Borderline* by Hanif Kureishi. Here the intricacies of cross-racial casting were added to the complexities of doubling, and it wasn't until nearly the interval that all the actors had appeared in their principal roles. Bill Gaskill's comment at an early preview was that the production didn't define itself early enough in the evening. We introduced a new first scene, all in Hindi, which took place at the Jullunder railway station, with the hapless emigrant saying goodbye to his family. It was a chaotic swirl of colour, noise and steam but it introduced the whole company and it established the rules of the evening with great force. Time is short in the theatre and a good production must lead its audience from the opening music.

# Tuesday, April 26th

## Dear George,

We've been doing the workshop for *Our Country's Good* for over a week now and I haven't found time to write. However, yesterday we were at the Theatre Museum in Covent Garden. We wanted to research eighteenth-century acting styles. What kind of acting would Lieutenant Ralph Clark have seen? What would the convicts have known of the theatre when they began to rehearse?

We saw prints of Anne Oldfield and Robert Wilks. Apparently Anne was your protégée, 'discovered' in The Mitre Inn, Covent Garden. And Robert Wilks (the first Captain Plume) was your friend from Dublin, at whose instigation you wrote *The Beaux' Stratagem*. We began to study Garrick's advice on posture and Macklin's on Attitudes. There set physical positions and gestures designed to convey particular states of emotion: 'Jealous Rage', 'Tranquil Joy' and even 'Voluptuous Indolence'. The famous picture of Garrick holding a dagger before him and with one hand on his brow must be a classic example of 'Tormented Rage'. Jim Fowler and Rhiannon Finamore from the Theatre Museum plied us with books. It seemed absurd to try and grasp in one day the detail that scholars had spent years researching. Here are some of the facts that flew by me in the morning: 'Quin used to saw the air . . . Betterton (1635–1710) was Master of his own acting school . . . actors took their own clothes along for comedy but not for tragedy . . . prejudice against actresses was deep-rooted in England; each had to win their reputation . . . a claptrap is a speech driven towards a fierce conclusion by the actor in order to obtain applause . . . each generation of actors tend to think of themselves as more natural than their immediate predecessors' . . . and finally a nice quote: 'Exaggeration clings to the second-rate actor in all periods.' (Alan S. Downer).

After a huge pizza and a glass of wine in Covent Garden with Mark Lambert and Jim Broadbent at lunchtime I had kind of

21

had it, and faced the afternoon with a great deal less clarity of purpose. What were we trying to pick up? In the Reading Room, which was exclusively ours for the afternoon, we began to rehearse some scenes from your play, basing them in part on the prints and portraits we had seen and partly on Macklin's Attitudes. It wasn't going very well. Linda, on whom I can usually depend for inspiration, in a tired moment had one of her occasional fits of fragmenting bottle and could do nothing. I think Alphonsia was having a rather tentative go at 'Voluptuous Indolence' when a gentleman who was also trying to use the Reading Room facilities, and who had been observing our struggles from a scholarly distance, came forward and introduced himself. Of course George, it turned out that Robert Hume, from the University of North Carolina, is one of the greatest living authorities on eighteenth-century drama and has written several books and monographs on you. He gave us a fascinating lecture on the whole subject of eighteenth-century theatre.

Apparently, things were going through a bad patch when you began your career in 1695: the court had withdrawn their patronage and theatre-going had not yet become a habit for the upwardly mobile middle class; it was felt that theatres were immoral and licentious and the plots frivolous; and Collier was about to publish his influential attack on the 'Immorality of the Stage'. I asked why so few playwrights from the eighteenth century have survived. Why couldn't I think of a single play written between *The Beaux' Stratagem* in 1707 and *She Stoops to Conquer* in 1773? Robert Hume said there were two principal reasons: first, in 1713 the Duke's Players and The King's Players combined to form The United Company, and with no competition there was no incentive to risk new work. Consequently, the United Company put on only revivals and no new plays were written. Secondly, it turned out that eighteenth-century theatre was a monument to enterprise economy. When *The Recruiting Officer* opened at Christopher Wren's Theatre Royal, Drury Lane, in 1706, the theatre seated 660, of whom 260 would have been servants in the galleries. During the course of the century, it was altered four times, each time seating more and more people, in order to maximize profits. It was finally demolished in 1791, and the new Drury Lane, which opened in 1794, accommodated over 3,600 people. The spoken word became lessened in value, the playwright disappeared, and theatre became dependent on the eighteenth-century equivalent of

22

*Chess* and *Starlight Express*. Stars and spectacle dominated the theatre. Your colleague, Congreve, was unperformed on the English stage for over 120 years and Garrick and Peg Woffington emerged as the first genuine theatre stars. Nor was Shakespeare immune. This was the time when *A Midsummer Night's Dream* was renamed *The Fairies* and when *King Lear* was given a happy ending. The disappearance of Royal patronage and the dominance of bourgeois taste was a disaster for the playwright. It's salutary to think that Drury Lane's expansive policies would have filled every criteria of the Arts Council Incentive Fund Scheme.

So it turns out that you were lucky, George. You were writing at a time when the bourgeois English public had hardly started going to the theatre and died before they were going in such numbers that they stifled its originality and verve.

## Dear George,

This is a letter about the workshop we've been doing with Timberlake for the last two weeks on *Our Country's Good* and I'm finding it hard to write. It's hard because a workshop isn't exactly rehearsal, nor is it journalistic investigation, nor is it academic research and yet it contains elements of all three of these. Part of the function is to familiarize and brief the actors, who are together for the first time. It's even more important to stimulate Timberlake and feed this research to her, for after this two weeks, she will begin work on a first draft. A workshop is often enjoyable because we're all temporarily released from first-night pressure. On the other hand, this can be replaced by an aimlessness and lack of focus. There is no script to centre the work.

We began by pooling our limited knowledge of the eighteenth century and we read a lot of books. Robert Hughes's *The Fatal Shore* was obligatory reading. This is a magnificent history of the early years of the Australian penal colony. Although it is unflinching in its history of a brutalized society, it is also a gripping account to which we shall no doubt return again and again throughout the workshop. We also depend on Roy Porter's *English Society in the Eighteenth Century*. Mossie brought in a book from her local library about the history of women convicts transported from Wales. The cast were shocked by Hughes's account of the journey of the First Fleet and the level of brutality the convicts endured. Norfolk Island became the San Quentin of the Australian prison system, with a régime so hideous that convicts entered suicide pacts to get off the island.

We began to grapple with the problem of depicting brutality on stage, and engaged with the aesthetics of cruelty. How can well-fed actors be starved convicts? How can you show somebody being beaten without it becoming hideous or prurient? How can we enter the world of such brutality?

Any improvisation reflects the knowledge and experience of

24

the actors undertaking it, and to begin with our work was tentative and shallow. I tried to address this problem by reading and working from Mayhew's books. His *History of the London Poor* is some fifty years removed from our period, but his studies and interviews of people scraping a living on the fringes of criminal society gave the actors a view of this harsh world from the point of view of specific characters. The interviews are detailed enough to base a case history on and, in the course of the two-week workshop, each of the actors presented one of these Mayhew characters to be interviewed by the rest of the group. Mark Lambert was James Mahon, who had been transported to Australia for housebreaking, but who had got his ticket of leave and returned. He was about to start thieving again and explained in detail how to break in through a fanlight. Alphonsia was a child prostitute called Nancy who was hooked on gin. Timberlake was particularly interested in canting talk and criminal jargon but I don't think we were able to give her much help with this one. The case histories were quite useful though, and they really came alive one afternoon.

Sitting round a large table in St Gabriel's Parish Hall I got the actors to recount their life stories – overlapping them several at a time . . . jump-cutting from two voices to all eight of them to just one voice for a moment. This gave great drive and energy to the session. It also stopped the actors thinking too carefully so they began to work more from instinct.

I use playing cards a lot, both in rehearsal and in a workshop, to focus the actors' imagination on specific points. Usually I begin with status games based on those developed by Keith Johnstone during his seminal work with the Royal Court's Writers' Group in the late 1950s. You define status on a scale of one to ten and, eliminating the court cards, choose a card at random. This number then becomes the actor's status for the scene. The actors' sole objective becomes to make their status as clear as possible. Thus an office-cleaner could be a ten while the executive, whose office is being turned upside down, could be a mere three. Cards can also define the warmth of emotional relationships: a couple on their first date choose cards at random which denote the extent of their relative passion for each other; or a whole history can be seen in the way in which a mother (eight) gives her son (four) a Christmas present. In the workshop we've just concluded, I began using cards to define and develop a particular argument.

There is a fairly early scene in the play set in the officers' mess at Sydney Cove where the whole merit of the proposed theatrical production is under discussion. The Governor General, Phillip, is a liberal, while the Senior Marine Officer, Major Ross, is quite vehemently opposed to the plan. Other opinion drifts between these two extremes. Timberlake was interested in hearing the different shades of opinion. The whole company chose cards at random. Any black card, spades or clubs, indicated opposition to the play, the strength of opposition being determined by the value of the card. Thus, a ten of spades meant that the actor had to marshal the arguments of a Mary Whitehouse. Red cards meant that you were a supporter of the scheme.

To begin with we rehearsed alternative debates. Should there be a smoking ban in rehearsal? This argument was resolved by the low reds and the low blacks pushing through a compromise resolution. We then debated contemporary questions of subsidy before moving the actors back two hundred years. We had various shots at this particular topic. I think it was always of more use in stimulating the company than it was in giving Timberlake any fresh arguments. But it was of great value in focusing the actors' imagination and passion. They became adept at marshalling arguments opposed to their own opinions. Jim Broadbent was funniest. I had begun to complicate the exercise by introducing characters. He was Ralph Clark, the young Marine Lieutenant, who had the task of directing the play. Each actor had to announce their character. Jim said, 'I'm Ralph Clark and I'm afraid I can't stay long, I've got a production meeting.'

We also used the cards to determine how good the convicts were as actors. We knew they should be a group of mixed abilities and, in this exercise, the value of the card simply indicated the acting potential of the convict. I set up scenes from your play, each with two actors and a director. The actors' observations of years of incompetent direction were hilarious: a scene where Mark Lambert was rather a good actor (eight) but forced to work on a scene with an untalented but enthusiastic Mossie Smith (five) and an incompetent director, Lesley Sharp (two), hit tragi-comic dimensions. We set up various audition scenes too, where the ability of the convict actors was also determined by the cards. Part of the value of these exercises is that it gives the actors a specific point of concentration that doesn't involve inventing a story or ornamenting a character. We also wished to explore the sensation of criminality. I set up a day-long improvisation, which took place alongside whatever else we were rehearsing: again roles were determined by cards, and whoever pulled the Jack became the thief, unknown to the rest of us. The thief then had to recruit a look-out before stealing as much as possible from the remainder of the company during the rest of the day. This made for a day of acute paranoia, but gave Linda Bassett the thrill of discovering evil at first hand.

Rolled-up newspapers, which look and sound like fearsome weapons but which don't hurt, were used in various games of brutality we devised. David Haig missed part of the workshop because of *Greenland* rehearsals. He arrived for the first time one afternoon and, within seconds, was stripped to his underpants and beaten enthusiastically by Mossie till he was glowing red and hauling stacks of chairs from one end of St Gabriel's Parish Hall to the other. In another game, the Three Lizzies, defined by Keneally as the hardest women in the colony, pushed their luck with a marine gaoler. The gaoler's alacrity and willingness to use force was again defined by a card. The Three Lizzies had to discover the value of the card without getting hit. It was like finding out how far you could go with a new master at school. Linda was brilliant at evading punishment but Mossie always seemed to miscalculate. On one occasion, imagining Mark's gaoler to be a wimpy four, she began a colourful rodomontade of insults. Linda and 'Phonsia had spotted that he was at least a manly eight and Mossie was left in splendid isolation, provoking a sharp crack on the thigh from Mark.

Throughout the two weeks, our knowledge of Australia and of the eighteenth century increased, and I'm sure this will also prove useful when we come back to your play again. Even in this short time the improvisations we undertook began to have more authority and confidence. One in which Mark Lambert was the amateur hangman learning the ropes and measuring Linda Bassett for the drop will find its way into Timberlake's script; although here again it won't be the words so much as Mark's tone of sweaty verbosity that Timberlake will pick up on.

On the last day, we set up a long improvisation in the sub-sub stage. Usually used as a store-room, this is a cave right underneath the stage amidst the foundations of the theatre. It looks like the bowels of a ship, with a low wooden ceiling, huge pillars and stout wooden struts. Here Mark went beserk, Jim ravished Alphonsia, David lashed Linda, Ron got cholera and was thrown overboard, and Mossie sold Lesley to Nick Dunning for an orange. It wasn't the invention so much as the atmosphere that made us heady. The improvisation had moments of fear and then moments of wild anarchic freedom.

We also met people during the workshop. This is always rewarding because it's so unpredictable. We wanted to meet some current convicts but we weren't able to set this up in time. We did meet a rather urbane recruiting sergeant from the 18th/19th Hussars. He told us that mothers were the recruiting sergeant's greatest enemy. David asked if there was tight male bonding in the army. (I think because of all the kissing between men you've observed, George.) Sergeant Major James replied tolerantly: 'Fortunately, in this world, everybody's different. . .'. His style was that of a reassuring and helpful bank manager. But Jim and Nick are going to spend an evening in the Sergeants' Mess when we start rehearsal again.

We also met a woman now working with the acting company, Clean Break, who had spent time in Holloway. She dreaded the psychiatric wing, which was called 'The Muppet House': 'Women shouting and screaming all the time . . . gets to you . . . I was banged up with a woman who dreamed she was going on a picnic and fucking her solicitor.' She talked compulsively about small injustices, and it was clear that, in an incarcerated society, these become obsessions. She had had her guitar confiscated by a screw. The details of the incident were vivid and clear. She talked of lifers, how 'some were brutal . . . others were broken from within . . .', a phrase that stuck in my mind. She told us how easy it was to become obsessed with work: 'You can really get into scrubbing and cleaning.' She gives a picture of female solidarity . . . men appeared to represent the more brutal world outside prison . . . and she talked of women who weren't really gay becoming 'prisonbent'. *The Fatal Shore* has a whole chapter on the convicts of Norfolk Island becoming 'prisonbent' too. Nineteenth-century bureaucracy meant the official reports could only squeamishly hint of 'unspeakable lewdness'.

Later I tried to set up some improvisations in the convict colony that had a similar focus on some small detail. We had some success. Linda was obsessed with the vicar's wife, for whom she worked, and who kept trying to be friendly with her. Jim was a boy who worked for a fisherman who had lost his job and so now couldn't go out in the boat. It was all quite good but not small-minded enough. I didn't push it through. I wish I had.

So, in the last two weeks, we've moved from collective ignorance to mass enthusiasm. We have digested information and the actors have begun to focus on an assortment of characters drawn from Keneally's novel and from other sources too. We spent the final part of the last afternoon discussing the elements from the workshop that we would like to see in the play. There was a very warm feeling, and Timberlake seems very clear about what is of interest to her. Still, it's rather a peculiar way of working and she hasn't done it before. The pressure will be considerable. The actors' enthusiasm makes for great expectations. She now has five weeks to begin a first draft before we start the official rehearsal for both plays. Next time the main focus will be on your play, although for the first couple of weeks we will be working with Timberlake as well.

## Dear George,

I had meant to confine my correspondence to
you entirely to the play. We start rehearsal in a month, but I
find myself unable to focus on it at all at the moment. Applying
for one's job wonderfully concentrates the mind, even as it
diminishes the spirit. I have been Artistic Director of the Royal
Court for over eight years now, and my current contract expires
at the end of next March. If I wish to keep the job I must re-
apply for it along with any other candidates. There has been no
great encouragement from the Royal Court Council for me to
do this. Indeed, my Chairman, Matthew Evans, has made it
clear that he feels it's time for a change. Obviously it's right the
Royal Court should have the best person for the job and it's
understandable that, after eight years, the Council wish to
examine their options, but this last winter's been a miserable
time. Not least because I wasn't sure how I intended to act. In
March, I received a letter from Matthew giving me a year's
notice. My name was spelt wrong. However, while I was in
New York over Christmas, I decided to go ahead and re-apply.
Fuck 'em.*

I think the responsibilities of the Theatre Manager would
probably be familiar to you. Later in the eighteenth century,
your fellow countryman, Thomas Sheridan, founded a theatrical
dynasty and did much to define the job of Artistic Director. His
management of Dublin's Smock Alley Theatre saw the banish-
ment of the audience from seats on the stage following the incident I mentioned earlier, involving Peg Woffington. He
increased press advertising for the theatre, stopped the custom
of half-price admission at the interval and even initiated a sub-
scription season ticket. Twenty-five years later, his son, Richard
Brinsley Sheridan, the great dramatist, had turned the Theatre
Royal, Drury Lane, into something of a family industry. His

*After two animated and penetrating interviews I was re-appointed.

wife, Elisabeth, was the Accountant; his father-in-law, Thomas Linley, was Musical Director; and his mother-in-law became Wardrobe Mistress. Much of the great Richard Brinsley's time was taken up with reading scripts, sending older plays for adaptation to dramatists and generally trying to find plays which touched the nerve and pulse of his time. Then, as now, this was a tricky task. Sheridan lived in an increasingly squeamish age, when much of the writing of your time, and even of Shakespeare's, seemed coarse and unrefined. Your work was okay, George; after all this was the time that Peg Woffington was to have such a success as Sir Harry Wildair. However your contemporary, John Vanbrugh, seemed too vulgar and R.B. Sheridan turned *The Relapse* into the more genteel *A Trip to Scarborough*. He also turned *The Tempest* into an opera (tunes by the father-in-law) and translated Kotzebue's *Pizarro*, giving large parts, which they repeated for the rest of their careers, to Mrs Siddons and Mrs Jordan. R.B. Sheridan's time as a Theatre Manager coincided with the expansion of the theatres, and it's ironic that one of Ireland's great dramatists helped establish England's first star system which did so little for the new generation of theatre writers.

How far should the Theatre Manager move to accommodate the taste of the town? Obviously, compromise is a dirty word, but we all swim in the same pool, and it takes a seer or a fool to defy the tide of popular opinion more than once in a season. Broadly speaking, committed theatre is becoming less fashionable in London at the moment and whoever is appointed as the Royal Court's Artistic Director may have to withstand the disapproval of fashion. London's current tide in theatrical chic is swinging towards groups such as Theatre de Complicité (enormously skilled absurdism) and to Cheek by Jowl (cheeky revivals of the classics). It's veering towards entertainment rather than to provocative debate. Plays that take on public issues may no longer carry the public with them. But as a political solution to the Left's problems seems increasingly remote, so the voice of theatre becomes more important. Its value in illuminating different corners of society and in explaining ourselves to ourselves has never been needed more.

As for the Royal Court, its position seems increasingly vulnerable. As public subsidy has dropped the theatre has become increasingly dependent on raising money. Over the last five years we've raised a higher proportion of our turnover than any other theatre in the country, except the National Theatre. But none of this diminishes the risky nature of new work and the volatile behaviour of our box office, despite record-breaking years in 1986 and 1987. In fact there's a danger that we've become so committed to incentive funding, marketing and fund-raising that it's become heretical to state what is obvious common sense, that without an equal commitment from the public sector, the Royal Court cannot continue as a major national resource for new writing. I favour compromise; I favour adding a judicious mixture of classics to the Royal Court's risky new work, but if you compromise and *still* remain unable to produce the work to which you are most passionately committed, then you must wonder what you are doing. Here are the words of a new playwright whose plays were ignored in favour of the classics: 'Is the credit of our age nothing? Must our present times pass away unnoticed by posterity?' This cry of agony comes from Oliver Goldsmith writing in the 1770s, when market forces had already swelled Drury Lane's capacity to 2,300, and when new writing had become too risky for the theatre manager to contemplate.

'Putting on new writing for the theatre remains at once the most risky and the most rewarding work,' wrote David Hare. This is always true. But it does occur to me that the job I'm about to re-apply for will be to guide the Royal Court at a time which will probably be the most risky and the most unrewarding in its history. It's no consolation to think that Richard Brinsley Sheridan died an alcoholic and in penury. But at least he found sponsorship on his deathbed. The bailiffs came to arrest him for debt, threatening to remove the bed itself and take him to prison, had not Whitbread, the brewer, arranged his timely release. Now, as then, people who run theatres need a friendly brewer.

# Sunday, 5 June

## Dear George,

I went up to Stratford yesterday to see *The Constant Couple*, directed by Roger Michell. Frankly, I never much enjoy going to Stratford; driving there is miserable, the icecreams are expensive and the reviews for *The Constant Couple* have been mixed. Also there are more unhappy and under-appreciated actors per acre in Stratford than anywhere I know outside Manhattan.

The truth is that most plays in the Stratford repertoire revolve round the crisis of the leading personality, e.g. Hamlet, but need rather a large company of actors to express that crisis. Few of the fifty or so actors in Stratford in any one summer get much focus. They certainly don't get the notices and, often, they feel they don't get much attention from the director either. When I met Peter Brook in New York (he's the most famous director of all of us, George), he said the one thing about a long rehearsal period was that then you could give equal attention to the smaller parts. Are actors' expectations higher nowadays? Something must rub off on an actor after working for years with Joint Stock, Common Stock, Shared Experience or General Will, even if only from the names. Actors do seem rather less happy playing smaller roles at Stratford or at the National than they used to be. Maybe that is because they have been rather more centre stage in the smaller companies.

Through the Seventies I led a touring company called Joint Stock. Inevitably I've brought some of the lessons I absorbed there with me to the Royal Court. One of the most important achievements of Joint Stock was to find a new way of presenting epic drama with less resources. At Stratford you expect to find twenty-two actors taking you through an evening, while with Joint Stock nine or ten actors will divide an evening between them. Joint Stock plays tend to place an historical event at the centre of the drama and then examine this moment

33

through the eyes of a range of people, rather than simply looking at it as a psychological crisis in the life of a single protagonist. In Caryl Churchill's *Light Shining in Buckinghamshire*, the
leading characters were played alternately by different actors,
which gave a greater sense of movement and sweep to the
events of the English Civil War. In fact, versatility became a
characteristic of Joint Stock's work. In Howard Brenton's
*Epsom Downs*, a company of nine actors played forty-nine parts
between them. But, in *Weapons of Happiness* by the same author,
at the National, twenty actors played twenty-two parts. Thus, as
always, economics dictate aesthetics. But, it's one thing to
fashion a play round a company of ten actors and quite another
to bend a classic to your will in the same way. On the other
hand, I'm sure you would regret it if the waning tide of our
resources left only the National and the RSC able to produce
your work.

Not surprisingly the casting requirements of *The Constant
Couple* and *The Recruiting Officer* are similar. There are also
footmen and a number of smaller lower-class parts in *The Constant Couple*. But with a large actor pool at his disposal, Roger
Michell's answer has been to provide a floating gang of beige-
suited footmen who play music, provide chairs and supply
props. They also become a chorus of disdainful and detached
observers. Not the least strange thing about the twentieth century, George, is that you would find a world without servants.

I thought the play was terrific, George. Very good work. You
wrote *The Constant Couple* at the age of twenty-two, didn't you?
So it would very nearly have qualified as an entrant in the Royal
Court's annual Young Writers' Festival. The play is observant,
incisive and has a sure grasp of character. Like *The Recruiting
Officer*, it operates both within the accepted form of conventional comedy and yet extends its range. I felt irritated that the
reviews had done such little justice to your work or to Roger
Michell's fine production. In Sir Harry Wildair, excellently
played this time by Pip Donaghy, you created a part which was
to be a top choice in every leading actor's repertoire for generations, and in Lady Lurewell you create a real original. At the
age of fifteen Lady Lurewell has been seduced by an Oxford
undergraduate to whom her father has shown hospitality. Consequently she harbours a bitter resentment against men. I've
noticed from *The Recruiting Officer* how explicit you are about
sex and money. What is shocking to us is, firstly, that Lady
Lurewell is so young when it happens and, secondly, that she

talks so directly about her seduction. In the world of Restoration Comedy we're accustomed to finding sex to be all vague gossip, innuendo, beauty spots and chat.

In some ways, Lady Lurewell's bitterness about men has its counterpart in Captain Plume's cynicism and misogyny in *The Recruiting Officer*. And yet, by the end of both plays, you lead your characters to recant these harsh opinions and redeem themselves by a warmer understanding of the opposite sex.

*The Constant Couple* seems to dwell rather more within the conventions of Restoration Comedy. That is, it implies there's a lot of sex going on. In *The Recruiting Officer* you give us possibly a more accurate picture. You tell us very clearly that all the women, with the exception of Lucy, are virgins. Melinda and Silvia discuss the vital subject of virginity in their first scene. Nor are the men necessarily very experienced. Plume has been through the Battle of Blenheim since he was last in Shrewsbury but, at the time of his last visit, he and Worthy must both have been more like boys than men. In their first encounter, they try to recapture the effortless male banter of the previous summer. Plume had courted Silvia but probably didn't get very far, and Worthy was making up his mind how seriously to take Melinda. Certainly Molly became pregnant as a result of a fugitive liaison that summer, and the town has talked of nothing else all winter; but it's probably quite near the truth when Plume tells Jack Wilful: 'I'm not that rake that the world imagines: I have got an air of freedom which people mistake for lewdness in me.'

And how sexually experienced would Worthy be? The opportunity to seduce a serving maid must have been there, but in the country you would have to live with the consequences of such impropriety. Nor would there have been much of a red-light district in Shrewsbury. So, maybe, the relationship and misunderstandings between Worthy and Melinda are the result of ignorance and fearfulness on both sides. This is all early speculation, uninformed by a working knowledge of the play, but it's clear that a quite proper preoccupation with sex and money characterizes your work. Obviously we must find out all we can about the relations between the sexes in your time. How closely were the moral precepts of the age followed? What were they exactly? Did anybody really mind that Plume made Molly pregnant? Justice Balance seems to turn a blind eye to this event, and I'm afraid, George, that you never let us have the opportunity to meet Molly herself. Above all, we must make the nature of the contact between the sexes as clear as possible.

Actually, George, I'm overawed. I didn't go to Stratford quite prepared for the prodigality of your talent. We start rehearsal tomorrow so I will be in touch regularly from now on. For the next two weeks we're working on *Our Country's Good* as well. Timberlake has written three scenes.

P.S.   There is a real footman problem though. With so few actors how do we move the furniture?

## Monday 6 June
### First Day of Rehearsal

## Dear George,

I am never terrified on the first day of rehearsal. At least you can always read through the play again and again. It's the third or fourth day that the honeymoon begins to wane. We read through *The Recruiting Officer* this morning. Everybody laughed a lot, which is always heartening. The actors were a bit insecure about the doubling. Linda Bassett was wonderfully touching as Thomas Pearmain but she hasn't yet persuaded herself she should play a man, while Ron Cook is concerned about the amount of time he has to effect the change between Bullock and Brazen. He would prefer to be seen as Brazen first, as this is his principal role. We didn't really confront the doubling problems in the last act this morning, although I think Nick Dunning may have to play the Constable. The problem is that there appear to be at least two occasions where he goes off as Worthy and has to re-emerge immediately as the Constable. I think this will probably be okay, although it's too unnerving a prospect to present to him just yet.

However, there does seem to be a real confusion here, in the twentieth century, about what kind of play you have written. Not amongst the actors, who were very happy this morning; but amongst the academics. Those I have been reading over the last few weeks are certainly divided both about the character of Plume and about your view of militarism. Eugene James (1972) believes that you demonstrate 'the immorality and cruelty of the military world', while Eric Rothstein (1967) believes your play is 'pro-war and is characterized by . . . dry-eyed, patriotic militarism'. Dr Peter Holland (1988) writes that 'the play is in no sense an attack on the war. . .' and says that you had no hesitation at all in supporting the war unequivocally'. While John Loftis (1959) says that only rarely are you chauvinist. I suppose that you yourself must have been confident of military approval because you didn't hesitate to dedicate the play to the Earl of Orrery, who had given you your commission. 'My recruits are reviewed by my general and my colonel, and couldn't fail to pass muster.'

All I can say, George, is that you're lucky not to be writing now, because I don't think the picture you give of Kite and Plume would pass much muster with the BBC. There's been much vexed correspondence in the *Daily Telegraph* about *Tumbledown*, the story of a young Guards officer hideously wounded in the Falklands War. The film, lucidly directed by Richard Eyre, charts the officer's increasing bitterness and cynicism in the face of bureaucratic ineptitude. Basically, *Tumbledown* is a pretty straightforward story. It shows once more how young men rush to war and find it terrifying and pointless . . . but the furore in the press has, in itself, been quite militant. The Brigade of Guards have protested to the BBC about the inaccurate picture of army life that has been given and, six years after the Falklands War, feeling runs high. Yet your play was staged within two years of the Battle of Blenheim, England's greatest land victory since Agincourt, and the sharp picture you give of military corruption did not lead to an outcry. Sure, Arthur Bedford attacked you in 'The Evil and Danger of Stage Plays' (1706). He thought *The Recruiting Officer* was unpatriotic and that it defamed the character of the nation's military officers. These are exactly the criticisms that have been levelled against *Tumbledown*. In 1706 Arthur Bedford was in a minority, but in 1737 the Lord Chamberlain and the Licensing Act were introduced to curb stage plays. In 1968 these powers were abolished, in large part owing to the campaign led by Bill Gaskill and the Royal Court. In 1988 the reaction to *Tumbledown* shows that we are once again entering a less tolerant age. The lesson is that these freedoms must regularly be fought for. The battle is never won.

What is certain is the impact and topicality the play must have had. I remember once again that you and your fellow Restoration dramatists were the first writers regularly setting your plays at the time you were writing, and in the place you were writing them. And that foremost among Restoration dramatists you set your plays against great contemporary events. The Jubilee of William and Mary in *The Constant Couple*, and the Battle of Blenheim in *The Recruiting Officer* are the great offstage events that dominate these plays.

So, with your concern for accuracy, what picture do you want us to have of Kite and Plume? Are they the dashing heroes of Blenheim or is there a darker picture of two men brutalized by a bloody campaign hastening back to the rustic haven of

Shrewsbury in the heart of England.

At least I'm getting a clear indication of what people would *like* to see. At lunchtime, Kate Harwood, the Royal Court's Literary Manager, showed me the prospective blurb for the Methuen playtext. It describes *The Recruiting Officer* as 'an effervescent comedy with one of the most rollicking first acts in theatre history'. Our own press office has an even jollier response: 'Two handsome grenadiers set about a major recruiting drive in a small country town.' This isn't quite the picture I have at the moment, although I appreciate the complimentary picture of David Haig and Jim Broadbent. I can see that, to a certain extent, Plume is a jolly careless fellow: a bit of a lad with the girls, not really wicked but a bit naughty; in fact a very attractive male stereotype, whose down-market male descendants can be recognized on TV today in *Eastenders* (Dirty Den) and *Brushstrokes* (Jacko). This could take Plume dangerously close to the conventional hero of Restoration drama. It's an unthinking stereotype we're all anxious to avoid.

What actions does Plume take in the first scene, which I will be rehearsing tomorrow? Well, he's first seen palming off his illegitimate son. Kite and Plume then agree to falsify the regimental records. He then proclaims his misogyny to his old friend Worthy, advocating various heartless and rather cruel courses of action for Worthy to take in his courtship of Melinda. Kite returns and Plume permits the depraved Kite to keep the ten guineas he has cheated from the unfortunate Molly. This had been a charitable gift from the kind-hearted but naïve Silvia, who is obviously obsessed with Plume. Is this a picture of 'an officer and a gentleman' that you have given us, George?

As for Sergeant Kite, his account of life in the army wouldn't even be allowed on Channel Four at three in the morning. He declares that he has learnt only 'whoring and drinking' in the army and that these qualities, together with 'lying, impudence, pimping, bullying, swearing and a halberd, the sum total will amount to a recruiting sergeant.' He appears to have started pimping at the age of ten. It seems to me a picture of a brutalized and disturbed psychopath. I don't think Norman Tebbit would approve, George.

I think the key relationships to try and pick away at first will be Kite and Plume; also Silvia and Plume. These two relationships seem the ones that drive the action. How close are Kite and Plume? Is it anything like a relationship today between officer and sergeant? How intensely were Silvia and Plume involved when he was last in Shrewsbury? When did Silvia find out that Molly was pregnant? How unusual is Silvia's determination to win Plume? On the one hand, it's a conventional theatrical device, but, on the other, it shows such passion and tenacity that when all is discovered she expects 'no pardon' from her father. (Interestingly enough, in Brecht's *Trumpets and Drums*, a play that, I'm afraid, has quite shamelessly gutted *The Recruiting Officer* and transposed it to the American Civil War, Silvia is turned into Victoria Balance, a schoolgirl with a crush on Plume, whom he can hardly remember from his previous visit. Is that obsession an insight on Brecht's part into their relationship?) How did men and women behave towards each other in public? Would they touch? If it were a play written today, Plume and Silvia would have commenced an affair on the previous visit. But we know that this has not happened. Hence, presumably, Plume's furtive and clandestine liaison with Molly at the Castle. Discovering the moral code will unlock the social behaviour, which will, in turn, illuminate the relationships.

As we start rehearsal of your play, there are two lingering ghosts I'm keen to avoid. One is described by William Gaskill in his book *A Sense of Direction*: 'At that time the words Restoration comedy meant high camp, lisps, huge wigs, canes and fans.' Because this is such a potent theatrical image and because also it is our only experience of the Restoration world, it's the magnet towards which all productions tend to be drawn. The other lingering ghost is, of course, Bill's own legendary production, which, in 1963, was one of the first done by the National Theatre at the Old Vic. I think, more than anything, it is the success of that production and the understandable fear of comparison that has kept your play off the London stage for twenty-five years. Ironically enough, I was in Dublin and didn't see it, but it was a formative experience for anybody of my generation who did. My own formative experiences with Bill came rather later. But, if these are the ghosts to avoid, what is the picture I'm keen to move towards? I didn't have a concept to offer the actors this morning – nor did they expect one – but if there is a picture in my mind, it's like one of those Rowlandson prints: a detailed teeming picture that shows a lusty, cruel and vital society. His cartoons always show a particular moment of drama; the moment a wig falls off or a glass slides to the ground. They're full of life and character but, above all, they depict the values and relations of their society with wit and with exactitude.

40

## Dear George,

Started in on money. We had all undertaken to read a chapter of Roy Porter's *English Society in the Eighteenth Century*, and the task was to summarize relevant chapters for each other. Not all actors make good teachers I find, although Alphonsia, who was a teacher before she became an actress, is a good disciplinarian. Mark dashes off at a tangent gripped by his own enthusiasm. It's probably best to start with you, George. We know that your commission as a Grenadier Lieutenant in the Earl of Orrery's Regiment was worth £54 15s. a year. Plume, in the superior rank of Captain, could expect roughly double that amount: £100 per annum. Roy Porter advises that multiplying eighteenth-century sums by sixty will give a rough and ready mid-1980s equivalent. On this basis, we were able to work out the enormous disparity in income of the play's characters.

By any standards, Melinda is very wealthy indeed. In fact, I think you have made her the wealthiest heiress in Restoration drama. Her £20,000 surpasses the £12,000 Congreve gives Millamant or the £1,500 per annum Vanbrugh allows Hoyden. Multiplied by sixty Melinda had inherited £1.2 million from her Aunt Richly in Flintshire. Porter tells us that one of the swiftest ways of making a fortune was from sugar. By 1790, £70 million had been invested in the West Indies. Could this be how Aunt Richly has made her money? It would explain casting Alphonsia, whose mother comes from Domenica, as Lucy. Maybe Melinda has inherited Lucy along with the money. There are several references in the play to the West Indies. Indeed, Brazen knew or had at least heard of Balance's uncle, who was Governor of the Leeward Islands. The enormity of this sum must have transformed Melinda's life completely. In fact, it may go some way to making her unhinged. She has no parents that we ever learn of. In fact she is completely unprotected. How can she believe a word any man says to her?

Especially the unworthy Worthy, who has formerly attempted to make her his mistress, simply because she wasn't wealthy enough to qualify as a wife. In his defence, it must be allowed that Worthy appears to have been ready to take Plume's advice and settle £500 per annum (£30,000) on Melinda. This seems generous to us, George; in fact, in our own rather less censorious times that kind of sum could secure you the services of almost anybody as a mistress. It also indicates that Worthy must be a man of considerable means. Melinda's insecurity with her new wealth, together with the vivid memory of her previous humiliations, enable us to speculate on the Plume/Melinda relationship.

They only meet twice on stage but Melinda seems vindictive towards the irresponsible Plume. She rightly suspects he has influenced Worthy.

> I warrant he [Worthy] had never been sober since that confounded Captain came to town; the devil take all officers, I say – they do the nation more harm by debauching us at home, than they do good by defending us abroad.

And Melinda is just the kind of woman to draw out Plume's misogyny. In fact, Plume's sourness and cynicism ('the world is all a cheat') must be driven by his impecunious situation. Here he is, clearly a gent and a hero of Blenheim, having to dupe dull country fellows. With an income in our terms of a measly £6,000 per annum he can have no great expectations of a match with Silvia (worth £72,000 per annum), as he himself accepts ( . . . 'I haven't the vanity to believe I shall ever gain a lady worth twelve hundred a year'). In fact, Balance is very liberal to consider him as a candidate for Silvia's hand. However, when she becomes the sole heir of his estate, Balance understandably feels this would be an appalling match from which Silvia must be protected. Porter estimates the average wealth of a peer of the realm to be £30,000, so it is no wonder that the ambitious Balance instructs Silvia that 'this fortune gives you a fair claim to quality and title': these were aims to be taken very seriously indeed.

Roy Porter is very good in helping us understand the underlying drives of the play: 'Young ladies were groomed with matrimony uppermost in view . . . it was not narrowly about the couple's happiness, but was a matter of family policy, securing the line's honour and fortunes.' Balance's determination to secure the inheritance of his estate is an objective that would have been immediately understood by your audience in eighteenth-century London, while we are in danger of misreading it. His behaviour is not that of an oppressive Victorian father but rather that of an unusually loving father concerned about protecting his daughter from the ruinous consequences of her declared and 'extravagant passion' for the indigent Captain Plume.

Porter is very specific about sex too: 'In polite society a lady's chastity before marriage, and fidelity after, were crucial for gentlemen.' Balance sees the danger of Plume's arrival in town: he knows of the affair with Molly ('there have been tears in town about that business Captain') and comes straight to the point in his fourth speech to Plume:

> Come come Captain, never mince the matter, would not you debauch my daughter if you could?

This shows admirable concern and pre-Victorian directness. In 1760, Dr Johnson wrote 'The chastity of women is of all importance, as all property depends on it.' Of course, Dr Johnson doesn't mean the chastity of working-class women, since no property depended on their keeping their knees clenched, and Molly stands at the gates of the play as a kind of warning of the perils of lost virtue. Dr Peter Holland writes: 'Plume does at least provide for his bastard . . . In terms of Farquhar's own society such actions are the least but also the most that a gentleman might be expected to do to deal with the consequences of an affair with a lower-class woman. While Plume's unconcerned irresponsibility must repel us, the response is not one the play seems to consider.' I suppose Peter Holland is right, George: the drive of the play is to make us side with the lads and see things from Plume's point of view. At least, the response to Molly's predicament gives us a clear moral signpost at the very start of the play. There's an even starker sentinel at the start of your first play, *Love and a Bottle*, where Roebuck, the dashing Irish hero, arrives in London pursued by Trudge, his Irish mistress, who has borne him twins but whom he refuses to marry or in any way provide for.

What about the finances of characters at the other end of the social scale? Pearmain and Appletree are freemen earning about 8d. a day (about £625 per annum today). No wonder joining up and becoming a gentleman seems such an attractive option.

And Plume's attraction to Rose is entirely tied to her perception of the economic potential of the relationship:

And I shall be a lady, a captain's lady and ride single upon a white horse with a star, upon a velvet sidesaddle.

Plume offers her a crown or £15 for a dozen chickens. Hardly a fortune, but she is overwhelmed at this offer.

So the characters at the bottom end of the scale are very poor indeed by contemporary standards. Again Roy Porter's book gave us confidence in this: 'Most of the working population lived below the breadline.' He quotes Gregory King (1688) as thinking that 'most family units in the labouring classes were irremediably in a poverty trap because they could not earn as much as they needed for subsistence . . . Everyone below the plateau of skilled craftsman was undernourished.' But important though it is to get the economic relationships right, I don't want to direct the play with the wisdom of Marxist hindsight. The poor are treated unthinkingly but not with wicked intention: 'Hardly anyone . . . not even most reformers and radicals doubted that there always would, or indeed *should*, be rich and poor; the dependent relationship seemed as natural as that between husband and wife or master and servant.' (Roy Porter).

Even at this early stage, it's possible to speculate on the superobjectives of some of the characters. By this, George, I simply mean their main goal over the course of the whole play, from which their other behaviour will spring. Balance's superobjective is to secure his estate while Silvia's is to secure Plume. Rose's is to rise socially, and Plume's superobjective could be simply to have a good time. If this is right, it explains why Plume is prepared to drop the idea of pursuing Silvia relatively easily. Although nobody would say that you write from the women's point of view, George, you do write very good parts for women and, moreover, at a time when 'women were laced tightly into constrictive roles . . . few escaped. The commonness of the stereotyping created a kind of invisibility; women were to be men's shadows.' (Roy Porter). Melinda's fiery vindictiveness and determination to punish Worthy is not just the flighty behaviour of a soubrette, it is the pre-feminist bitterness of a young woman who has seen the abyss into which she has nearly been tumbled. Shrewsbury must have been a town that 'marched to the strict drum beat of the community's values. People were continually in the public eye and censure was shameful and disabling.' (Porter). So, although I don't think you intend us to see Plume as villainous in his behaviour to women, or Balance as wicked in his behaviour to the working class, you have written the play with a particular sensibility to the situations in which women and poorer people found themselves.

The humour of the play comes partly from the wit of the language, but it will be even funnier if we can make the reality of the social situations come alive. The research will help but I wish I was a bit more learnèd. I'm having to read at top speed just to scratch the surface. Jonathan Miller seems to have history as well as art at his fingertips. I'm just not very well read. Still, a good day in which we grasped some eighteenth-century realities about both sex and money.

P.S. Slept well.

## Dear George,

I would understand if you had become upset by my passing reference to Brecht's *Trumpets and Drums*, but I can reassure you that we won't be incorporating any passages from it in our production. Indeed, George, I must convince you that I am not so serious a socialist as to wish to simplify the complexity of art with the certainty of dogma. I do realise that Brecht has turned your play inside out and I fully understand how upsetting it must be to find, for example, one of Bullock's speeches re-allocated to Sergeant Kite. I know you must be familiar with the idea of adaptation. I understand that re-writing and re-working old plays was a major industry for writers in the seventeenth and eighteenth centuries. Then as now audiences had a preference for older plays or, at least, for particular versions of them; so filleted and rearranged versions of Shakespeare, Jonson, Beaumont and Fletcher were the staple basis of any Theatre Manager's annual repertory. And I understand you yourself tried your hand at the odd adaptation, turning a French farce into *The Stagecoach*, to become a popular afterpiece, and also re-working Fletcher's rather tedious *Wild Goose Chase*, transforming it into *The Inconstant*. This played in the season of 1702 without much critical success. Nor did it pass without comment from your contemporaries; it inspired this rather hurtful couplet:

His fame he built on mighty Davenant's wit
And lately owned a play he never writ.

It's strangely familiar to hear that, with all this adaptation going on, writers complained with vigour that their work was being excluded because of the timidity of managers unwilling to take a risk with a new play. The irony is that, after your death, *The Recruiting Officer* became the most revived and popular play of the next fifty years and together – in order of popularity – with

*Hamlet*, *The Beaux' Stratagem*, *Macbeth* and *The Beggar's Opera*, was a hardy perennial in the repertory of both Drury Lane and Covent Garden.

But I would agree that Brecht's adaptation is a bit of a mess. Indeed, I would say that it is, at best, a clever comment on your play rather than an original work in its own right and that it is doomed to become an unstudied footnote in dramaturgical history. What interests me is the teaming and specific picture of Shrewsbury life in the summer of 1705 (I'm not sure about the exact dating of the play, but will write to you later about that). Brecht moves the play forward fifty years to the American Civil War, which is thus seen as a staging post in the epic struggle for class freedom. Any ambivalence in behaviour is ironed out, and Balance becomes a totally unscrupulous and corrupt figure of the establishment. Brecht's Plume ceases to have any complexity of motivation and becomes simply a wriggling opportunist who sponges on the breathy schoolgirl, Victoria (Silvia), and is finally hustled into marriage only by Victoria's trickery and the prospect of an increased marriage settlement from the two-dimensional Balance. Worthy becomes a shoe manufacturer, eager to secure the contract to supply Plume's recruits, and Melinda becomes diminished to the point where I do not believe it could be a role that Dame Linda Bassett would even consider taking up. The charm, robust sexuality, vigour, earthiness and incidental cruelty of your original are all transformed into the spiteful, selfish, cynical sniping of the class war.

On the other hand, it must be acknowledged that Brecht focused attention on your satire of small-town life, and prepared the way for a more accurate and complete view, which had become obscured by Restoration camp. Certainly, Bill Gaskill acknowledges as much when citing reasons for choosing the play for the National in 1963. And, although Marxist theory doesn't explain every single aspect of human behaviour, it's probably true that an approach to your play that didn't mess about with the text but, nonetheless, chose a superobjective for each character, determined by class interest, would lead to a pretty well-muscled production. Maybe that's the way we ought to go. There is also the odd quixotic touch by Brecht that I think even you would appreciate. I have already mentioned Silvia's transformation into a schoolgirl; another is the outrageous inclusion of a favourite Brecht song 'Seven Reservists from Z Battery', here allocated to Plume to sing while he's shaving. Finally, there's Brecht's intention, stated in his plan of the play, that Plume will become a stockbroker in the City on leaving the army 'and [will] multiply Melinda's twenty thousand pounds for her.'

But Brecht's version is casual. For a Marxist to update the period of the play but update only *some* of the sums of money, leaving others as they stand, thus preventing any financial overview of the world he creates, seems sloppy and careless.

We're heading fairly slowly into the text, still spending a lot of time discussing and familiarizing ourselves with eighteenth-century history. More about rehearsal tomorrow.

*A Director Prepares.*

*Working on the train to Shrewsbury. L to R: David Haig, Max, Jim Broadbent, Nick Dunning.*

*Shoemakers Row, Shrewsbury, leads down to the Market Square where Sergeant Kite makes his recruiting speech that opens the play.*

The company in Dr Dudley Ireland's Queen Anne House, completed in 1710.

Linda Bassett in Dr Ireland's garden overlooking the Severn. For our production this became Justice Balance's house.

*The Riverside walks where Melinda pursues Worthy, and where Plume and Brazen fight their duel.*

*Mardall. Jim Broadbent had him down as Costar Pearmain or Tummas Appletree. If you're singing with a guitar outside Boots you're certainly possible recruiting material. I was less sure; he was playing Dylan songs.*

*Two shopgirls in the doorway of Boots. This is where the hapless Molly, made pregnant by Captain Plume, might be working today.*

*The Prologue: the idea of restoring the sideboxes at The Royal Court came from this Rowlandson print.*

*Rowlandson: Scene off Spithead. Obviously they're not she-lags, but this print always made me think of the convict women being shipped aboard the transports of the First Fleet.*

*Rowlandson's print of Mrs Siddons rehearsing in the Green Room at Drury Lane. These gestures indicate 'attitudes' or 'states of mind' and we drew on them when we rehearsed THE RECRUITING OFFICER scenes in OUR COUNTRY'S GOOD. The actor in the background is rehearsing in front of a mirror. Dated 1789, the year of the convict production.*

*Strolling Actresses dressing in a barn. Published 1738.*

*Linda Bassett dressing in a Royal Court Dressing Room.*

# Friday, 10 June

### End of First Week's Rehearsal

## Dear George,

Slow progress, I'm afraid. In fact, I always unnerve myself by how very slow progress is at the start of rehearsal. I've been thinking about your play for months, but now we're in rehearsal the immediate inclination is to hustle straight through it in order to get a grasp of the whole. No less a director than John Dexter customarily has a run-through at the end of the first week's rehearsal, I'm told. Nonetheless, I prefer to creep up on the play rather than assault it. So we have sat round a small table in the upstairs rehearsal room at Hampstead Theatre all week. It's a nice rehearsal room. It's got windows, and I have egg, bacon and chip lunches at the community café across the little square. I lunch alone – it seems easier to fret by yourself – and join the others on the mound between the library and the theatre at the end of the lunch hour. The weather is good.

During the week, a pattern emerges and we discover more about each other. Jude and Jim travel by bike. Jude is the one who will be late for rehearsal, if I don't stop him now. David's baby girl wakes him early in the morning and he's performing at night, so it may be good not to call him too early. Nick Dunning eats nuts and is, I think, a vegetarian.

I begin rehearsal, after the first day, by analysing each character's intentions and breaking them down into 'actions' line by line. More about 'actions' later. But it's a slow way of working and will probably take us the best part of three weeks. The historical detail is equally important and should inform every decision we take. There are dangers though. It's easy to fear a glib, unresearched production, but it's equally possible to leave the best work in the rehearsal room and not apply the research to the text. There's no point in discovering how upper-class women behave towards lower-class men or how Justice Balance would treat his maidservants, if there's no opportunity to show these relationships onstage through your lines.

At the same time as working through the play and discovering the 'actions' or intentions, we've begun to make some discoveries about the characters. Although not all the company are in the first few scenes, this is work I do with everybody at 2.00 p.m. each day. Sometimes, I take a word: nervous. Who feels nervous? Plume feels nervous at meeting Silvia after nine months away. He talks about that and explores it. Will she still fancy him? Will she sleep with him this time? Will she mention marriage again straight away? (She does.) Rose feels nervous at talking to Plume. He appears to fancy her, but as a well brought up farm girl ('Have a care, Rose, don't shame your parentage,' warns her brother, Bullock), she is worried by his overtures. She is attracted to him but well aware of the social gulf between them. Worthy too is nervous. Nervous at finding himself alone with Sergeant Kite. His relationship with the lower classes has, customarily, been structured and well ordered, while the anarchic and brutalized Kite is alarmingly out of place in Shrewsbury Market Square; 'Why thou'rt the most useful fellow in nature to your captain, admirable in your way, I find,' proffers Worthy tentatively.

So, it's been an exciting week, George, although the principal discovery has been the extent of our ignorance. I'm also wondering about Kite and Plume's relationship. My image of the relationship between an officer and an NCO comes from Second World War films via *Beyond the Fringe*. Is it more like the brotherhood of two villains? Do they like each other or is that irrelevant? Is Kite both butch and gay? I know the men kissing each other doesn't necessarily mean everyone in the army is a homosexual, but, at the same time, Kite doesn't seem to have much time for women, and the army would certainly be the place where both power and young men were readily available. I wonder if you liked the army? Perhaps it didn't represent the establishment in quite the same way it does now. Certainly it must have been less structured. David Haig has lent me a book by John Keegan, a military historian. I must read that over the weekend.

# Saturday, 11 June
## First Weekend

*Dear George,*

This is the last two day weekend I shall have for the foreseeable future and I'm afraid I became distracted spending most of today reading Lieutenant Ralph Clark's journal. I felt bad because it's not strictly pertinent to your play except that it did give me a day out in the eighteenth century. So this letter concerns the personality of the director of your Australian premiere.

Lieutenant Ralph Clark's journal has been published by the Library of Australian History and the copy my assistant, Mel, ordered from Sydney arrived last week. It's a day-by-day account of the five years spent by Lieutenant Ralph Clark, Royal Marines, in Australia and was written to show to his young wife, Betsey Alicia, on his return from service abroad. He sailed from Plymouth on the First Fleet in May 1747 and was in Sydney when *The Recruiting Officer* was produced in June 1789. Keneally's novel is a skilful blend of fact and fiction, and his pleasant fiction is to make Clark the director of the convict production. In fact, references to the production are scanty in the officer's journals and the real director remains unknown. I think Watkin Tench's journal makes a passing reference to the production having gone off quite well. Ralph Clark's journal is quoted in some detail by Robert Hughes in *The Fatal Shore* and the character Keneally has drawn is based on the fearful creature who emerges from these diaries. It was a shock today to make the man's acquaintance first hand. He is a haunted, homesick subaltern, anxious about money and concerned about promotion. His very ordinariness is extraordinary. I spent the earlier part of the year rehearsing Brenton's play about Byron and Shelley; men who were in every way exceptional. Byron's letters are among the most witty and urbane ever written. His descriptions of Greece, Italy and Albania show the eighteenth-century mind at its most engaging and inquisitive. His near contemporary, Ralph Clark, arrives in Australia but his curiosity remains in Plymouth, worried about his wife's ability to

51

manage the household finances in his absence. His dreams are a sweltering pre-Freudian jungle of fantasy and repression:

> 28 June 1787: dreamt of being with my beloved Alicia – oh why did the dear sweet woman learn me to believe in dreams if she had should not have been so unhappy as I am at tis present moment from dreaming that my Alicia took a dead louse from herself and gave it to me – oh unlucky dream for have often heard her say that dreaming of lise was a certain sign of sickness

He keeps Betsey Alicia's picture encased in a bag. Every day he kisses the case and every Sunday removes it and involves the picture in his obsessive ritual. The entry is surrounded by more mundane matters:

> Sun 29 July 1787: hope soon to be into port where we may have fresh Beff again – opened the case of my dr. Beloved Betsey's pictour and gave it a hunder kisses dear Sweet woman for herself and my dr Boy . . . the convict woman finished the pair of Trousers that I gave her to make and they fit very well.

But it is the disturbing presence of the twenty-seven convict women packed into the hold of the *Friendship* as they swelter southwards on their 8,000-mile journey that really finds out the chinks in Ralph's personality. Neither his life in Devon nor service in the Marines have prepared him for his duties guarding these women. Most were in their early twenties and, although some had been transported for stealing as little as 1s. 6d., there were doubtless some pretty tough and brutalized criminals amongst the terrified women. Within three days of sailing, he is blaming the women convicts for discontent among the crew:

> 16 May 1787: I never met with a parcle of more discontent fellows in my life they only want more Provisions to give it to the damed whores the convict Women of whome they are very fond since they brock through the Bulk head and had connection with them. I never could have thought that there wair so many abandond wretches in England, they are ten thousand time worse than the men Convicts and I am afraid that we will have a grate dele more trouble with them.

Later the pressure he is under makes him even more vicious and vindictive:

5 July 1787: . . . Capt Meridith order one of the Corporals to flog with a rope Elizah. Dudgeon for being impertinent – the Corporal did not play with her but laid it home which I was very glad to see – then order her to tied to the pump she has long been fishing for it which she has now got untill her hearts containt.

But he records the abusive cursing and screeching of another convict woman, who is being ordered into leg-irons, with a horrified fascination:

18 July 1787: . . . in all the course of my days I never herd Such exspertions come from the Mouth of human being She hoped and she was certain that she should see use all throne overboard before we got to Botany Bay. She disired Meredith to come and kiss her C. . . for he was nothing but a Lousy Rascall as we Wair all . . . I wish to god She Was out of the ship – I would reather have a hundred more men than to have a single Woman – I hope in the ships that ever I May goe in herafter there may not be a Single Woman.

Even Ralph's attempts at wit at the convict women's expense comes across as sour. At Cape Town the women were transferred to another ship:

5 Nov 1787: . . . 30 sheep came on board this day and wair put in the Place wher the women convicts were – I think we will find much more Agreeable Ship mates than they were.

He later records the death of some of these sheep with more compassion and pity than he ever shows for the convicts. What with the damned whores of women by day and his terrifying nightmares each night that caused him to cry out loud for hours on end, his only recorded solace appears to be in reading plays:

10 July 1787: Read the remainder of the Tragedy of *Douglas* this oh it is a Sweet play . . . what are the emotions in the Breast of Lady Randolph when She Sees the features and shape of her lost and Stained Husband Douglas in that of

young Norval – little dose she know fond Mother that he is her long lost Son.

The first volume of the diaries covers the voyage and arrival in Australia ('one of the worst Countries in the World'). Volume Two of the journals is missing and covers the period when *The Recruiting Officer* was being produced. The third and final volume was written when Ralph was stationed on Norfolk Island. The diaries contain no reference to Mary Brenham, the she-lag by whom Ralph had a daughter and with whom he lived for at least eighteen months of his posting. Keneally casts her as Silvia in the convict production. The lack of reference is not surprising, given that the diaries were intended for Betsey Alicia's eyes in Plymouth . . . but what were the emotions in the Breast of Ralph Clark, we are entitled to wonder, when he saw the features and shape of His Daughter and convict Wife for the last time as he sailed from Sydney Cove in November 1791? His daughter was named Betsey Alicia. What did Mary Brenham (aged nineteen) think of that? The events seem so extraordinary and the moral leap so bold that we have no way of judging it.

Did Ralph's relationship with Mary soften his attitude to the convict women? It would be sentimental to read too much of a change into his behaviour, but the entry for June 1791 does at least contain an element of curiosity about the women he was still lashing so blithely. It was yet another of the many Lizzies who sailed on the First Fleet:

6 June 1791: . . . Elizth Pipking to receive 25 lashes for disobedience of order for Coming Into Town without Leave – she could receive Six as she faintd away – it is a thousand pittious that She is abandoned woman for She is in figure a fine woman and has got a handsome face.

But the entry that made the hair stand up on the back of my neck is quite simple and was made during Ralph Clark's return voyage to England.

6 May 1792 . . . Last night the child beloning to Mary Broad the convict woman who went a way in the fishing boat from Port Jackson last year died about four o'clock committed the Body in the deep.

Mary Broad, or Braund, is the Dabby Bryant of Keneally's novel and her escape from Sydney, with three children and five male companions, ranks with Captain Bligh's as one of the most extraordinary voyages ever undertaken in an open boat. By an amazing chance she was re-arrested in Cape Town and was being shipped back to Newgate to await a further trial for escaping when Ralph made this entry. Keneally records that she was befriended by Boswell, who petitioned the Admiralty for her pardon. Her sensational history attracted public attention and she was reprieved and returned to her native Fowey, where she lived to be an old woman. Boswell gave her a pension of ten guineas a year.

It's these facts about the convicts that are so gripping. Robert Sideway *did* found Australia's first professional theatre when he got his ticket of leave. Mary Brenham *did* have Ralph's child. Dabby Bryant *did* escape and Ralph Clark *did* have nightmares. With *Serious Money* the workshop involved us meeting people working in the City and inhabiting their lives as accurately and as imaginatively as possible. It involves research of a different nature to get in touch with Ralph Clark and Robert Sideway, but is no less fascinating.

# Sunday 12 June
## First Weekend

*Dear George,*

Got back to *The Recruiting Officer* today.
Am I right in thinking that the play is set in the autumn of
1704? We know that Plume's earlier visit to Shrewsbury was
nine months previously, as Molly has just been brought to bed
of a chopping boy when the play begins. And I gather that, like
the cricket season, military campaigns took place in the summer
when the weather was good. The winter was spent in recruiting
and securing cash and supplies. The Battle of Blenheim was
fought on 13th August 1704. The end of the season. The
weather was humid and hot. Marlborough attacked the Franco-
Bavarian forces, who had cut off his army supply lines.
Although not as fearsome as the 'very murdering battle of
Malplaquet', a scene of terrible cruelties ('The Butcher's Bill'),
the casualties at Blenheim were bad enough: about one-third of
the eighty thousand troops engaged on both sides suffered
injury. Flintlock muskets, much superior to the old matchlocks,
would have been used; and hand-to-hand fighting with swords,
as well as artillery rounds and cavalry charges with sabres and
lances, increased the casualties. It involved the largest number
of troops ever to be engaged in modern battle and the news of
the victory was sensational. Marlborough was still on horse-
back when he scrawled a message in black lead pencil on a scrap
of paper and gave the dispatch to his aide, who rode for eight
days non-stop to give the news to Sarah Churchill at Windsor.

As for Plume, how did he feel during that hot, sticky night of
12th August, when he made his will, leaving everything to the
young woman he had met in Shrewsbury the previous year? 'As
contact with the enemy draws near, anticipation sharpens into
fear. Its physical effects are striking. The heart beats rapidly, the
face shines with sweat and the mouth grows dry – so dry that
men often emerge from battle with blackened mouths and
chapped lips. The jaws gape as the teeth chatter, and in an
effort to control himself, a man may clench his jaw so tightly

that it will ache for days afterwards. Many lose control of their bladder or their bowels.' (John Keegan, *Soldiers*). So, there's Plume, sleepless, smelling of his own shitten breeches, his sweat staining the paper on which he writes. He must have left Shrewsbury soon after Christmas 1703, following his plaintive autumn romance with Silvia and his furtive but steamy liaison with Molly. The Battle of Blenheim ended that summer's campaign and, released for recruiting duties, Plume makes straight for Shrewsbury, sending Sergeant Kite ahead of him. He arrives there by the middle of September, barely a month after the battle. It is a blissful early autumn with fine weather, which of course enables you to set over half the scenes in your play out of doors, either in the Market Square or in the Walk down by the river. This makes sense of Balance introducing Plume as 'a gentleman from Germany'. He's come almost straight from the battlefield. What does this do to the playing of those early scenes? It means Worthy, Balance and Silvia must all be overwhelmed with relief and pleasure at seeing Plume 'scaped safe from Germany'. Plume himself tells Worthy that he has 'lost neither leg, arm nor nose'. This is news worth telling indeed when there was a one in three chance that he might have been killed or maimed. Also, what heroes he and Kite must be! If ever there was a chance that Plume could seduce Silvia, he has it now. No wonder Balance has to make a swift pre-emptive strike and send her out of town ('I'm glad my daughter's gone fairly off though'). And no wonder Plume and Kite hit the bottle to celebrate their return ('I warrant he [Worthy] has never been sober since that confounded captain came to town' says Melinda). Plume doesn't even want to talk about the battle; even when pressed for 'a particular description of the Battle of Blenheim' by Balance, he eludes the question. ('The battle, sir, was a very pretty battle as one should desire to see, but we were all so intent upon victory that we never minded the battle.') This is the voice of someone not eager to recall the horrors of war for cocktail party chat just yet.

I've been reading John Keegan's extraordinary book, *The Face of Battle*. It's not about Blenheim but it's a reconstruction of Agincourt, Waterloo and the Somme from the soldiers' point of view. It's a shock. Most of the troops on both sides at Waterloo were drunk. Lifeguardsman Shaw, one of the heroes of the battle, was 'guzzling gin at about noon' and was 'drunk and running amok' when he was cut down by the French cuirassiers. As for Kite, if he had been there, 'his glorious halberd' would probably have been used to prevent his own side's troops from running away. Keegan records that a painting by Germaine Lejeune depicts 'a French sergeant pushing against the back of one of the French ranks, using his halberd horizontally in both hands to hold the men in place. It's not improbable to think of British sergeants having done the same at Waterloo', nor indeed to imagine Sergeant Kite doing the same at Blenheim. Plume appears to have real hopes of becoming a professional soldier and, at least twice, mentions his hopes of becoming a general. It was in the eighteenth century that the army became gentry-led, and the profession of soldier became respectable, particularly for younger sons. And, of course, fortunes could be made; Marlborough ended up a multimillionaire and was given the Palace of Blenheim by a grateful nation. In fact, by the end of the war, people began to suspect he'd made rather too much money out of it. That's probably why Wellington ended up on the £5 note rather than Marlborough.

So, where does this leave Plume and Kite? After the Battle of Blenheim, they're entitled to forget the horrors of war and have a fairly relaxed time in Shrewsbury. I begin to feel confident about the two superobjectives we've been heading for last week. The tentative decision we made was that Plume's is to have a good time and Kite's is probably to make as much money as possible. (He should be counting it in between each client in the Fortune-Telling scene.) Any 'actions' (full explanation will follow, I promise) for a particular line or intentions for a scene should be related back to these overall superobjectives.

Is *The Recruiting Officer* just a country comedy? Am I reading too much into all this military stuff? I can't see that I am: after all George, why should people assume that you don't know what you're writing about? You had been a serving soldier and, although you weren't at Blenheim, most biographers believe your ma's story that you were present as a boy-soldier at the Battle of the Boyne and that you were in Derry during the siege. It doesn't seem wrong to read an awareness of the shock of battle into your writing.

Ah well, it's ten to two on Monday morning and I've been reading and writing since *The South Bank Show* finished. My mind's racing and I could go on all night; but, in fact, I feel a bit queasy . . . I love the weekends . . . but I always feel apprehensive going back into rehearsal on Monday morning . . . and there's not much worse than starting the week exhausted.

# Monday 13 June
## Start of Second Week's Rehearsal

## Dear George,

Quite difficult today to switch from your play to Timberlake's work-in-progress and focus on Keneally's novel. During the last week, the actors have become quite fired with *The Recruiting Officer* and are anxious to work it through completely: breaking down the script into actions and intentions. I too feel tantalized. After a week we've just reached Brazen's entrance in Act III, Scene 1, but it's vital to do some more work with Timberlake while the ideas are still fluid. Thomas Keneally is in town and spent the morning with us in rehearsal. He divides his time between Sydney and New York where he has a teaching post. He rang last week to say he was sorry he couldn't spend more time with us 'but I'm head down and arse up in this new novel I'm writing'. I think you would like him, although I'm not sure you would approve of his wife's family. Three out of her eight great-grandparents were transported from Ireland.

I don't think he knows much about the theatre but he enjoyed the social situation in the rehearsal room, and he talked fluently and wittily for most of the morning. I was aware, while we were talking to him, of the liberties we will be taking with his novel. The real problem Timberlake has is in compressing and selecting from the many different strands in *The Playmaker*. A less generous man might have more qualms, or perhaps I mean a more knowledgeable one. How is he to know what we're up to when we barely know ourselves? He was, of course, particularly helpful on Arabanoo and the aborigines. The confused and touching relationship between the liberal Governor and the first captured aborigine is a successful theme in the novel.

Keneally said that the fence, as much as whisky or infected blankets, had killed the aborigines, by breaking their song lines. At first they imagined the white invaders were fallen stars, and they had difficulty in discerning the correct gender of the whites they met – particularly with the smooth-shaven officers.

Hence the order, recorded by both Keneally and Robert Hughes, for the odd Jack Tar to lower his strides and reveal his manhood to the confused aborigines. He talked about the shifts in morality between your time and ours, and the hastier life cycle. Dabby Bryant had been convicted, transported, escaped, recaptured, re-imprisoned, pardoned and was back in Fowey by the age of twenty-eight. The impact of serial childbirth shattered a woman's life.

He talked of the real people behind the characters in the book. Robert Sideway's theatre was closed down by Governor Hunter. Harry Brewer had been an embezzler but he had some skill at draughtmanship and he drew the plans for His Excellency's first house. The more individual officers (Davy Collins, Watkin Tench) adapted better to the peculiarities of the convict colony while poor Ralph Clark never flourished. I realized the respect with which the officers of the First Fleet are held by Australians. 'If Australian history does have captains and kings then Tench and Collins are among the captains,' Keneally said. He told us that Australian feminists had had a field day at the expense of Ralph's journals, but Keneally thinks he 'was just a poor narrow-minded neurotic . . . I wanted him to do the play because I so liked his dreams.' As for the voyage of the First Fleet, 'horrific though it must have been, it was also a triumph and I think it must have had an effect on convict morale. His Excellency made sure they got their vitamins.'

It was a good day and once again it confirmed the immensity of our ignorance about the subject we're undertaking. There's only one subject in which I feel confident of my comparative grasp as it were and that's over *The Recruiting Officer* itself. Here Tom's vision is rather a romantic one. He uses the play in the novel as a wonderful love story the power of which propels Ralph Clark and Mary Brenham together. He describes the play almost like an intoxicant. Redemption through sexuality, or, to be more accurate, redemption through Romantic Love. Well, certainly David Hare would go along with this. His theory is that the most profound and transforming experience most people go through in their lives is Romantic Love. Ralph Clark's story can only be about the power of romance if you halt it (as Keneally does) at the point when he falls in love with Mary Brenham/Silvia. The naming of their daughter Betsey Alicia after his wife, and his return to Plymouth abandoning his New World family turns the real history into a kind of Triumph of Pragmatism.

But there's no denying the sheer sensuality and Romanticism of the theatre and the power it has over those who come in touch with it. It is almost like a sexual attraction. Keneally certainly sees this; and so did you, George. *The National Dictionary of Biography* has it as a fact that you had an affair with Anne Oldfield, your first Silvia. In fact, there's probably been no sexier period in theatre history than the Restoration: actresses on stage for the first time and titillating subjects discussed there too. Nell Gwynne, a comedienne rated highly by Samuel Pepys, climbed the highest social pinnacle – into the King's bed – while Lavinia Fenton, the first Polly Peachum, became Duchess of Bolton. So, no wonder the power and sexuality of theatre is so feared by Major Ross and his supporters in the officers' mess. Their alarm is a real one. The disgust and contempt for the convict women outlined by Ralph Clark in his journals is the prevailing and fiercely held opinion: they are vile and unspeakable whores deserving only punishment and contempt. As soon as they become actresses they become legitimate and attainable objects of sexual admiration. There becomes no reason why one shouldn't get off with His Excellency himself and become Duchess of Sydney, as it were; thus creating a power base that would certainly undercut Major Ross.

So probably the obsession of our own age with actresses won't come as a total surprise to you, George. The affairs of actresses and the misbehaviour of actors are still headline news. And Marilyn Monroe and Joan Collins are still our principal icons of sexuality. As for me, I have been stage-struck for as long as I can remember. My granny took me every year to the panto at the Lewisham Hippodrome. Whether it was *Aladdin* or *Babes in the Wood* or *Cinderella*, the first scene was always dancing on the village green, and it always featured the Lewisham Babes in attractive mock peasant outfits. The promise they gave was of a world of shining hair, sparkling smiles and high heels. It probably won't surprise you, either, to learn that the principal boy is always played by a woman and that most pantomimes feature a man *en travesti* playing a comic older woman character. I loved this world without reservation, and its magnetism drew me into the theatre.

# Tuesday 14 June
### Rehearsal Week Two: Act III Sc. ii

## Dear George,

Back to *The Recruiting Officer* today. We've got as far as Act Three Scene Two which is the first scene set on the walk by the river with Melinda and her maid, Lucy. The scene went easily and the relationship between the two women seemed very real. Lucy is a superior servant and Melinda is tetchy with her because, as she reveals in the next scene, she really wants a confidante and friend. Sometimes she treats Lucy warmly and, at other moments, with frigid hauteur. We defined Melinda's objective as being 'to talk about Worthy' while Lucy's is 'to keep Melinda happy'. Melinda is lacking in self-confidence. She is insecure at the relative eccentricity of her position – as an independent but unprotected woman of means. Linda Bassett relates to Melinda's neurosis and finds the balance between comedy and unhappiness easier than we did last week in the first meeting between Silvia and Melinda.

However, I'm finding it harder than I imagined to locate the women's position in society. It's easy to slip into a priggish tone and condemn the manner in which women were treated in your time, George, but there is a casual mixture of sensuality and brutality that makes one queasy. Even though it's at the wrong end of the century, there's a Gillray cartoon that illustrates the point. A clamp-down on public gambling offences in 1797, when the Lord Chief Justice had announced that anyone 'whatever may be their rank or station in the country' would be punished, prompted Gillray to draw the topless public flogging of Lady Buckinghamshire. The cartoon depicts a plump and sensual lady, with osprey feather hat, leaning forward with her hands tied in front of her. Her fashionable dress is hoicked down to her waist and the marks of the lashes are already apparent on her shoulders and arms; behind her a bewigged Lord Chief Justice lays it home with cat and birch. Under his upraised arm, a grinning and jostling public look on.

Ralph Clark's alarm and terror at the female convicts in his charge has already been noted, as has Plume's cynical and dyspeptic attitude. Yours was certainly a tough century for a woman. 'Public life was a men only club.' (Roy Porter). Even the language was tough on women: any woman who slept with a man before marriage was his whore. You show this cruel side of the eighteenth century most clearly in your first play, *Love and a Bottle*. Your hero, Roebuck, explains that he has had to leave Ireland because he made a girl pregnant:

Roebuck: My unconscionable father, because I was a Rogue in Debauching her, wou'd make me a Fool by wedding her; But I wou'd not marry a Whore, and he would not own a disobedient son, and so . . .

Lovewell: But was she a gentlewoman?

Roebuck: Pshew! No, she had no fortune . . .

Lovewell: But what necessity forc'd you to leave the Kingdom?

Roebuck: I'll tell you. To shun the insulting Authority of an incens'd Father, the dull and often-repeated advice of impertinent Relations, the continual clamours of a furious Woman, and the shrill bawling of an ill-natur'd Bastard – From all which, Good Lord deliver me.

Lovewell: And so you left them to the Grand Dada! Ha, ha, ha.

Roebuck: Heaven was pleased to lessen my affliction, by taking away the she Brat; but the t'other is, I hope, well, because a brave Boy, whom I christen'd Edward, after thee, Lovewell.

This echoes the early conversation in *The Recruiting Officer* between Plume and Worthy. But it is particularly hard on your supporters, George, as later in the play, Lyric, the impecunious writer, explains that 'the hero in Comedy is always the Poet's character . . . and as the Catastrophe of all Tragedies is Death, so the end of Comedies is Marriage.' Many apologists have sought to exonerate you from all this, by making out that it's rash to assume the characteristics of the hero to be those of the writer himself. This is, of course, quite true. Often a writer romanticizes or distorts his own characteristics. For example, the central character of a recent play in the Theatre Upstairs, was an attractive, articulate liberal – stallion-like in his virility – whose chief activity in the play was to make love endlessly to an Australian nurse. It was hard to imagine the rather taciturn author featuring in a similar real-life drama. Plume, Roebuck and Sir Harry Wildair all have a certain macho aggression and a confident swashbuckling sexuality. Indeed, Roebuck is obsessed with sex. On his first visit to London he stares out of the window in amazement at the fashionable crumpet in the streets and he later appears in a tavern with 'six Whores and a carted Bawd'. We can only guess how far you shared Roebuck's rapacious sexual curiosity. But there are two experiences that we know for certain you do have in common with Plume, Roebuck, Archer and Aimwell: one is a first-hand acquaintance with poverty, and the other, of course, is that you are all outsiders. You and Roebuck were new boys in London, and Plume is a stranger to Shrewsbury, as the two gents in *The Beaux' Stratagem* are strangers in Lichfield. Plume is able to enjoy Shrewsbury as a privileged outsider without being tied by its social obligations: hence the particular danger that Plume represents and to which Balance responds.

But am I banging on about women too much? I suppose it's hardly surprising that women are treated almost as a separate species in the eighteenth century and that no play, even those written by your contemporary women writers, make women the protagonists and instigators of their plays. Aphra Behn, Mary Pix, Mrs Manley and Susannah Centlivre all enjoyed some success as dramatists. Mrs Centlivre was your exact contemporary (she was writing from 1700 to 1724) and you would have been particularly struck by how *The Busybody* and *'Tis a Wonder a Woman keeps a Secret* took the town. I reckon that Mrs Centlivre treats sex roles fairly conventionally, but that great authority and Female Wit, Fidelis Morgan, assesses her contribution highly. Interestingly enough, the editor of your collected works believes that you had a liaison with Mrs Centlivre and that some of your poetry was originally addressed to her. So, it was a time when, at least in France, the salons were established and, among the intelligentsia, women began to question their roles. But the shadow of a holocaust must have affected men's relationships with women in the eighteenth century, even as our relationship with the Jewish community is now shadowed by the events of the Second World War. The ghastly tide of witch-hunting had reached its peak a century before the Age of Reason but it's been estimated that around nine million women were killed in Europe over the preceding three centuries. In Hugh Trevor Roper's words: 'the hideous reservoir of hatred which seemed to be drying up, was suddenly refilled.'

It's no wonder that the embers of this sex war still seem to us too hot for comfort . . . But how much of all this is relevant? How much can be brought to bear on your play? More to-morrow on what *we're* up to and on the rehearsal process.

# Wednesday 15 June
## Rehearsal Week Two: Act III Sc ii

## Dear George,

Finished Act Three today, which is steady progress. We're going through the whole play, breaking it down into objectives and actions. We should get through it by the end of next week (the third week of rehearsal). This seems an awful long time to sit round a table with pencils and rubbers, but I find that this way of working gives us a basic structure. I'm coy about revealing my working method to you, because it's a bit personal and I would imagine it'd be easy to sniff at. I think all good directors have evolved their own way of working, cobbled together like mine from things that have worked. I certainly didn't start with a theory, nor do I feel in the least messianic about it, but I do feel protective. I've never actually studied Stanislavsky but I'm sure this is a Stanislavsky-based working method. *Méthode Stanislavskoise* so to speak. It depends on yoking together instinct and analysis and using them to plough the text. Let's take the short scene between Silvia (here disguised as Wilful) and Kite, that we worked on today, and which will end the first half. We have said that Kite's superobjective for the whole play is to make as much money as possible and that Silvia's is to marry Plume. This morning we defined objectives for this particular scene. Kite's was to seduce Wilful/Silvia, whose own objective was to fend off Kite. With these particular objectives in mind, the scene is then broken down into 'actions'.

An action has to be expressed by a transitive verb and gives the character's intention or tactic for that particular thought. For example, if I was speaking to you at this moment, George, my overall intention for the scene might be 'to teach George'. Along the way the actions I would employ could be 'to interest', 'to grip', 'to instruct', 'to fascinate' or even, and here I would be a bit ambitious, 'to enthrall'. The fact that I could fail with these glorious intentions, and in fact end up puzzling or confusing or even, heavens forbid, boring you, is not my problem as an actor. That's not my intention. One definition of bad acting would be when an actor plays the result of his action (e.g. 'bores') and not the intention itself (e.g. 'educates' or 'interests'). It's up to the other actors in the scene to play the response, not for the protagonist to act a judgement on himself. So, here's how this small scene looked when we had first added in the 'actions':

BRAZEN *takes* PLUME *to one side of the stage and entertains him in dumb show*

**Objectives for the scene: Kite wants to seduce Wilful, Silvia wants to fend off Kite**

Kite: **Befriends** – Sir, he in the plain coat is Captain Plume; I'm his sergeant and will take my oath on't.

Silvia: **Warns** – What! You are Sergeant Kite?

Kite: **Pleases** – At your service.

Silvia: **Snubs** – Then I would not take your oath for a farthing.

Kite: **Disarms audience** – A very understanding youth of his age. **Intrigues** – Pray, sir, let me look you full in the face.

Silvia: **Suspects** – Well, sir, what have you to say to my face?

Kite: **Flatters** – The very image and superscription of my brother, two bullets of the same calibre were never so like; **Pressures** – sure it must be Charles, Charles –

Silvia: **Challenges** – What d'ye mean by Charles?

Kite: **Binds** – The voice too, only a little variation in effa ut flat; my dear brother, for I must call you so, **Inveigles** – if you should have the fortune to enter into the most noble society of the sword, I bespeak you for a comrade.

Silvia: **Halts** – No, sir, I'll be your captain's comrade if anybody's.

Kite: **Praises** – Ambition! There again, 'tis a noble for a soldier; **Encourages** – by that I gained this glorious halberd. **Flatters** – Ambition! I see a commission in his face already; **Grabs** – pray, noble Captain, give me leave to salute you.                      *Offers to kiss her*

Silvia: **Spurns** – What, men kiss one another!

Kite: **Jollies** – We officers do, 'tis our way; we live together like man and wife, always either kissing or fighting – **Focuses** – But I see a storm a-coming.

Silvia: **Dares** – Now, Sergeant. I shall see who is your captain by knocking down t'other.


Having pinpointed the actions, we read the scene through, announcing each action before actually reading the line: Jim began by saying 'Kite befriends Wilful' before relating his line. Having road-tested the actions, we were then in a position to amend and correct them. Obviously it's no good saying 'Kite charms Wilful' if, in fact, his instinct takes him in another direction as soon as he acts it. In this particular case, it was hard to see who was running the scene. Silvia/Wilful's actions bespoke a confidence that seemed out of place for her first attempt to convince as a man, while Kite's actions seemed at variance with his declared superobjective of making as much money as possible. We looked at the scene again and Kite's intention for the scene became 'to recruit' Wilful rather than to seduce him. Silvia's changed as well and became to convince Kite. This still involved a certain amount of fending off as Lesley Sharp was terrified about getting too close to the canny Kite. With these changes in emphasis we went back and re-examined the scene, changing some actions, but by no means all. The discarded actions and objectives are left in brackets where they have been changed.

BRAZEN *takes* PLUME *to one side of the stage and entertains him in dumb show*

**Objectives for the scene: Kite wants to [seduce] recruit Wilful, Silvia wants to [fend off] convince Kite**

Kite: **Befriends** – Sir, he in the plain coat is Captain Plume; I'm his sergeant and will take my oath on't.

Silvia: **[Warns] Distances** – What! You are Sergeant Kite?

Kite: **Pleases** – At your service.

Silvia: **[Snubs] Amuses** – Then I would not take your oath for a farthing.

Kite: **Disarms audience** – A very understanding youth of his age. **Intrigues** – Pray, sir, let me look you full in the face.

Silvia: [**Suspects**] **Fears** – Well, sir, what have you to say to my face?

Kite: **Flatters** – The very image and superscription of my brother, two bullets of the same calibre were never so like; **Pressures** – sure it must be Charles, Charles –

Silvia: [**Challenges**] **Discourages** – What d'ye mean by Charles?

Kite: **Binds** – The voice too, only a little variation in effa ut flat; my dear brother, for I must call you so, [**Inveigles**] **Charms** – if you should have the fortune to enter into the most noble society of the sword, I bespeak you for a comrade.

Silvia: [**Halts**] **Mollifies** – No, sir, I'll be your captain's comrade if anybody's.

Kite: **Praises** – Ambition! There again, 'tis a noble for a soldier; **Encourages** – by that I gained this glorious halberd. [**Flatters**] **Reassures** – Ambition! I see a commission in his face already; [**Grabs**] **Binds** – pray, noble Captain, give me leave to salute you.          *Offers to kiss her*

Silvia: [**Spurns**] **Cheers** – What, men kiss one another!

Kite: [**Jollies**] **Alerts** – We officers do, 'tis our way; **warns** – we live together like man and wife, always either kissing or fighting – **Focuses** – But I see a storm a-coming.

Silvia: [**Dares**] **Diverts** – Now, Sergeant. I shall see who is your captain by knocking down t'other.

To a certain extent, the original actions still hold good; there remains a certain sexual overtone to Kite's friendliness, and Silvia's determination to convince Kite is accompanied by an even greater desire to keep him at a distance. Nor did the scene appear to lose anything in comic richness. As always when we find an even greater level of reality it gets funnier: Kite's warning about life in the army ('We live together like man and wife') is more amusing when it's a real indication of likely conditions.

Working with agreed actions means that each actor knows and subscribes to a particular shape to the scene. It certainly shouldn't be treated as a rigid working method but it does establish a common language. In this company there's nobody who resists it, thank God.

Mossie Smith's range of transitive verbs is a bit eccentric, 'flaps off' is her favourite at the moment. When we come back to do a scene again in a week or so's time the actions will probably have changed. That doesn't matter. It's not a rigid plaster cast that will encapsulate the scene forever, but rather a first-stage rocket designed to fall away once the scene has been launched into orbit. It treats analysis as a more formidable tool in cracking a scene than instinct. This is something American actors often find hard to accept. But truth to tell instinct is employed all the time too. Each time we re-play the actions the actors are acting and reacting instinctively to each other; analysing this instinct and correcting the actions, even though they're still sitting round a table. It also means that the first stage of rehearsal is both intimate and intense. It is divorced from any attempt to stage the play, so that, the practical and necessary compromises – e.g. how can I kiss her if I'm wearing a sword? – don't intrude at this point. All that will happen later. If we've 'actioned' a scene while still sitting down and it's gone well, I may occasionally try moving it – just using chairs and boxes, without taking any real decision on either moves or furniture positions. This helps stimulate thought in that direction. Ideally, the transition from rehearsal room table to staging the play should be·as seamless as possible. Of course, it never is.

The actors are doing very well. Mossie Smith has caught Rose's innocent sexual enthusiasm. Ron Cook is superb as Bullock but is puzzled by Brazen. Lesley Sharp has a line on Wilful but hasn't caught Silvia yet, and David Haig has a proper military tone. Mark Lambert is a Dubliner and somewhat perverse casting as Justice Balance, the English establishment figure. He isn't playing high enough status just yet,* nor has he got the firmness of the moral stance. I reminded him of the card games we had used and asked him to mark his status from a six to a nine.

It seems good and we're enjoying it. Directing a play is a bit like mending a car. It's a pragmatic art: you keep trying things, eliminating some faults, testing again, trying something else,

*See 2nd May, p. 25.

but the *sine qua non* is confidence in your ability to make it go. At the best of times that comes and goes, but it's here at the moment. Still rehearsing at Hampstead, sunny weather. I walk over Primrose Hill most mornings.

How does all this compare with rehearsal conditions in your day, George? On the first day of rehearsal the author customarily read the play to the assembled actors in the Green Room. Some playwrights were poor readers of their own work; Dryden was notoriously tedious. While others were rather too good. Nathaniel Lee read the characters he had written so well that one actor 'threw down his part and said "Unless I was able to play it as well as you read it, to what purpose should I undertake it?" ' Where did you stand? Having considerable experience as an actor (I understand you played Othello in Dublin), I imagine you read *The Recruiting Officer* with feeling and wit. Although the affair with your protégée, Anne Oldfield, was probably history at this point, she must have been delighted to hear the wonderful role you had written for her. They were a company you knew well and presumably felt relaxed with: as well as your best friend from Dublin, Robert Wilks, who was to play Plume, there were four other members of the company who had been in your very first play, *Love and a Bottle*, four years earlier. A graceful and extraordinary compliment to one of the company is contained in the text: the role of Bullock, a country clown, was to be played by William Bullock. Bill Bullock must have been pleased to have been preserved for posterity.

What happened after the read-through? In 1708 you usually rehearsed plays for four weeks: so do we. Your critics and drama instructors laid much emphasis on proximity to nature, and so do we. One big difference though is in the number of roles actors were asked to play in one season. Highfill calls it 'a terrifying repertoire' and records that in 1791–2 John Fawcett acted 38 different characters and spoke 'a dozen prologues on 109 nights'. This meant that not all the four weeks designated for rehearsal were devoted to rehearsing the one play. Directors working with the Royal Shakespeare Company now are familiar with actors having multiple calls on their time and focus.

I reckon conditions deteriorated as the eighteenth century progressed and the intimacy and humanity of the Restoration stage gave way to the vast Hippodromes of the early nineteenth century. I have done some more reading since our day in the Theatre Museum and find that theatre became a huge commercial venture by the 1780s. Enormous profits were made at

71

London's two patent theatres and new plays became too risky. 'One thing is certain: these audiences went to the theatre for *Amusement.*' They delighted in comedy rather than tragedy; 'old comedies altered to suit the taste of the times' were the order of the day. (Harry Pedicord). The number of weeks spent in rehearsal grew less rather than more as making a profit became the vital imperative. Sir Walter Scott wrote an essay in 1819 on the decline of serious dramatic writing in Britain, and Byron was invited onto the Committee of Drury Lane as a kind of dramaturg to find some intellectual respectability for what had become an increasingly lowbrow operation. He commissioned a translation from Coleridge that was not delivered, and had a brief affair with an actress in the company. She wrote him some plaintive and rather moving letters. But the tide of history was against him. All this confirms my belief that beyond a certain size the theatre loses its power to provoke and becomes a medium for entertainment only. Comedy becomes farce, tragedy veers towards melodrama, and both become dependent on scenery and spectacle.

The whole style and approach to acting must have changed as theatres became bigger. Height and stature became attributes for an actor. Garrick, a small man, began to lay aside heroic roles like Othello, and Highfill cattily records that 'beautiful Margaret Cayler . . . advanced under Sheridan's management largely because of her Junoesque proportions.' An ability to project became essential and the English actor's obsession with voice and with technique was born. Not everybody took easily to these traumatic changes. When Drury Lane re-opened in 1794, Mrs Siddons continued to speak and perform as she always had done albeit, as one contemporary critic wrote, 'at a disadvantage . . . in that she is not everywhere heard. To be so she would strain her voice unnaturally. She does not choose to make the sacrifice, and preserves her excellence to the near, whatever she may lose to the remote.' A few playgoers were aware of what had been lost in the name of progress. Lord Torrington was one: 'Restore me to the warm close observant seats of Old Drury . . . the nice discrimination of the actor's face, and of the actor's feeling are now lost in the vast void of the new theatre at Drury Lane.' The writers suffered most. After all, not many new plays would be produced today if they could only be performed in the Olivier, the Barbican, or the Palladium.

A whole craft and a relationship between actor, audience and material was lost for generations. It's no accident that our present-day vigour in theatre writing was led in 1956 by two theatres – The Theatre Royal, at Stratford East and at the Royal Court – that approximated in size to the old Restoration theatres. Nor is it an accident that George Devine reduced the Royal Court capacity. Built in 1888 to seat 730 people, successive managements have reduced the capacity to its current 397, an interesting reversal of eighteenth century Drury Lane. It has become an exact space able to present epic theatre with intimacy or domestic drama with passion. Subsidy makes a theatre of this size economic. But if we were to be entirely dependent on market forces, theatres would grow in size once more. Very shortly somewhere like the Theatre Upstairs will either cease to operate, or will be subsidized by the actors themselves – working for nothing in order to practise their craft and create a showcase so they can get real jobs. This happens already in New York and in Los Angeles.

I suppose I'm trying to imagine the conditions under which your actors rehearsed and acted, and the relationship they had with you and with each other, so that we can both re-create those conditions and understand how the play worked. Ten days ago, on the first day of rehearsal, I said I didn't have a concept of the play, it was certainly true. I think this is the nearest we will get to a credo and may be all we need.

# Thursday 16 June
## Second Week of Rehearsal

*Dear George,*

Beginning to feel confused trying to direct two plays at once. Spent time today organizing research that still needs to be done for *Our Country's Good*. Divided the actors into teams. Nick Dunning will walk from Southwark to Drury Lane; accompanied by a map of eighteenth-century London and Mark Lambert. They are to report back on what they would have seen rather than what they see. I think Timberlake has it in mind that Robert Sideway (to be played by Nick) – pickpocket, theatre connoisseur and true Londoner – will recollect the glory and taste of London on the far Australian shore with the same feeling that Joyce recalled Dublin. Mark is to play Ketch Freeman, Australia's first hangman. How does he research that? A visit to Madame Tussaud's? David and Jim are to go to the Maritime Museum at Greenwich in order to find out about promotion in the Royal Navy and Wardroom/Officers' Mess rituals and behaviour. Jim plays Harry Brewer, who is the oldest midshipman in the Navy. Lesley and Mossie have to penetrate a Young Offenders' institution. Nick Dunning's sister is a social worker and could help. Mary Brenham (Lesley) is not a hardened criminal – she's just nicked clothes from her employer and betrayed his trust. I can't focus Lesley. She wants to research everything and may end up finding out nothing. She offers 'I would be possibly quite interested in meeting a white witch.' Well, wouldn't we all. Linda and Alphonsia are the tough team assigned to prisons and drug addicts. Something will come out of this research but probably not what we're expecting. Timberlake seems chirpy. On Monday we're going to Shrewsbury for a day out. I believe in research, just as Stanislavsky believed in sense memory or emotional recall to stimulate and release the actors' imagination. Wish you could come with us, George.

We're fast approaching the Fortune-Telling scene in Act Four of your play which looks a little tricky to me, George. Do you think a cut or two would be in order? The structure seems repetitive with two jolly Salopians, a butcher and a blacksmith, visiting the disguised Kite, before the plot resumes with Melinda and Lucy's visit. Michael Colgan, who runs Dublin's Gate Theatre, had a big success with *The Recruiting Officer* two years ago. 'One tip,' he says. 'Cut the second half.' Well, I wouldn't take a producer's advice without examining it pretty carefully, but I have a hunch something needs trimming. It seems the narrative drive sags a bit. But I'm a bit nervous of the scene altogether: how much of it is germane and how much is superfluous funny business? I've never directed Shakespeare but when I do, I shall find the lowbrow comic scenes the hardest. Beware the tavern scenes. How convincing is Kite? If he's playing his superobjective then he has to make as much money out of each punter as possible. He says as much in the first scene 'This device, Sir, will get you men, and me money which I think is all we want at present . . .'

We pooled our knowledge of the occult and about fortune-telling this afternoon and attempted various improvisations. Mossie set one up which replayed an extraordinary incident that had happened to her some years ago. She plays a taxi driver and Lesley plays Mossie. She gets into a taxi at Victoria to go to the BBC in Acton. The driver examines her in the rear-view mirror and tells her he has a message from Harry. Lesley – that is Mossie – freezes. 'It's okay,' the driver explains, 'he's fine and pleased you're doing so well.' The driver drops her at the Acton Hilton. 'Sorry love it's just something I've been able to do these last few years. I didn't mean to shock you.' It turns out Harry is Mossie's dead father. It's chilling and powerful. I ask how much tip she gives the driver. It was £5. But the lesson acting-wise is how little Mossie has to do once her authority is established, and how committed to believing her Lesley becomes. We do some more improvisations. In one, David Haig is a genial but barely competent fortune-teller at Camden Lock. But what's wonderful is how quickly he's able to find out what Linda wants to hear, from her responses to the cards he deals. The improvisations aren't revelatory or very original, but they do show the mechanics of fortune-telling and its potency. I feel much more confident approaching the Fortune-Telling scene. Interestingly enough, George, it's one of the few scenes in the play which you felt needed the help of props and business to establish an atmosphere. You write 'Kite disguised in a strange habit sitting at a table whereon are book and globes'.

75

After rehearsal, back in the Royal Court for a production meeting. I arrive late. Everybody gloomy. It appears the set and costume budget is £6,500 adrift. The costs have been severely underbudgeted for a period drama: the wigs alone will cost over £2,000. Every year as increased subsidy fails to match inflation, there's less money for actually putting on plays. This year £25,000 less. So, in order to produce as much as last year and not cut back, we've had to take some fairly imaginative budgeting decisions. So far they haven't come off. The Brenton season was optimistically budgeted to take 55 per cent cash. In fact, *Bloody Poetry* took 30 per cent and *Greenland* may not even do as well as that. So that the context in which we need an extra £6,500 is that we're already heading towards a likely £30,000 deficit on the year. Peter Hartwell is cross and despondent. He's being asked to design a major classic with a woefully inadequate budget. *The Recruiting Officer* is relatively safely budgeted to take 50 per cent cash. What should we do? If I push the anticipated income up to 55 per cent we will have 'created' an extra £5,000. But we've been caught out doing this already this year.* I prolong the discussion but, in the end, do what I know we have to do: save £1,500 from elsewhere in the budget, mostly sound costs, and agree to an extra £5,000 expenditure. This isn't rash, it's necessity, but with five weeks till we open the current advance is only £550. It's a bit early and this isn't too ominous, but the public aren't exactly rushing the doors just yet.

I like money. I think it's interesting. So, when people say 'Oh you're not directing a play at the moment, so you must be worrying about money – how awful for you', I correct them. No art can exist in an economic vacuum, but there's a real danger at the moment of worrying too much. The Royal Court's long- and short-term problems are considerable. The short-term ones at any rate will be much relieved if *The Recruiting Officer* is a huge hit, but I mustn't allow myself to feel that pressure too much. I should stop thinking about it till we open on 26th July. At least we'll have some costumes now. At one moment this evening a wigless, bejeaned modern-dress production seemed a tangible possibility.

*In the event *The Recruiting Officer* played to 59% cash and 71% attendance.

# Friday 17 June
## End of Second Week's Rehearsal: Act IV Sc. ii

## Dear George,

In the morning we worked on *The Recruiting Officer*, heading into the unknown reaches of the Fortune-Telling scene, and in the afternoon we had one of our final sessions on *Our Country's Good* before Timberlake produces a script. Next week we focus on *The Recruiting Officer* exclusively. Mossie had interviewed the criminal element in her local pub. She's surprised how willing he is to talk about his life once he learns she's doing a play, and she's also surprised at her own sense of purpose: 'Normally, I would be scared.' He's working as a temporary barman but he's a petty thief who has done time in Ford Open Prison. He 'hated doing the fucking gardening . . . I mean what do I know about digging holes.' This rang true. The First Fleet convicts were useless gardeners and would rather starve than learn to be farmers. He also said he started thieving, 'because I was fucking hungry, that's why.' This struck chords too. His first theft was goods worth £11 from the local supermarket. We discuss whether this sum would have got him transported.

We did some more work on the moral attitude the Marine Officers would have had to Ralph Clark's production of your play. Timberlake confirms that there will be a scene in the Officers' Mess, where they discuss the merits of theatre. How many officers can we have? Ten, if the whole company play officers regardless of gender, or six, if only the men are in it. Keneally has emphasized how tangible and well documented was the animosity between Major Ross, who was the Senior Marine Officer (a part I know Mark yearns for), and Governor Phillip. Once again, the strength of each character's support or opposition to the production is determined by the cards; red for support, black for resistance. Only this time characters are allocated and the actors themselves selected a card appropriate to their role. It worked out like this: Davy Collins red four, Governor Phillip red nine, Watkin Tench black three, Robbie

Ross black ten, Ralph Clark red ten, Dick Johnson black three and so on. It didn't work much better than it had last time. The actors weren't in touch with the passions that would ignite the debate. I tried it differently: instead of a group debate, each actor sat on a single chair, facing the rest of the group, and articulated their position. This gave some formality and prevented the exercise turning into general conversation. It was better but still not brilliant. I abandoned Australia and brought it nearer home; mindful of our trip next Monday, I made the actors citizens of Shrewsbury. Should the council give money to the local dramatic society? There was no professional theatre within a thirty-mile radius. The argument began to come alive. I changed the rules again; now the actors pulled cards at random, went up to the chair, became a Salopian and expressed the point of view determined by the card.

To start with the black cards were predominant and there was a drizzle of opposition. Ron was a brilliant black four. He reckoned some people thought they ought to have a few bob but he felt the local angling club had more support and deserved help to clean up their stretch of river and clear it of eel pollution. After all, what was Shrewsbury famous for? Its river, not its amateur theatrical set-up. Then Lesley Sharp, with a high red, gave a radiant and heartfelt speech in favour of theatre. She described being part of the Shrewsbury Players; the excitement of the group and how thrilling it was for her to run the coffee bar for the dramatic club. We became energized as we all began to recall and respect our amateur origins. Ron had become a professional actor because he had received timely encouragement from his headmaster at college. Of course, Ralph Clark's actors are all amateurs and must begin to find and uncover their own abilities in the course of rehearsal. How heady, in a society where your own self-esteem, accomplishment and worth are zero-rated, to begin to discover the excitement of play-making. I think Stanislavsky would call these exercises Emotional Recall, and Uta Hagen, in her book *Respect for Acting*, calls chapters on similar exercises 'Substitution' and 'Emotional Memory'. Although the afternoon's work may seem indulgent, George, it served both to give a first-hand experience of the actors' feelings about their profession, and to put the actors themselves in touch with their own passions. None of us can possibly know what it was like to be a convict in Sydney Cove in 1789, but we all remember what it was like on the first occasion our emotions were gripped by the theatre. The cards themselves and the structure of the exercise became irrelevant once we had discovered what to release. The afternoon showed that we still have problems in marshalling the range of arguments Timberlake would like for the officers, but that the feelings of the convicts are well within our grasp.

*Dear George,*

About the Fortune-Telling scene, which seems a comic excursion that is in danger of becoming disconnected from the main story. . Of course, I accept that funny business is germane and equally important for the entertainment of a diverse house. At the same time, I still think the scene needs some editing. I rather suspect that your original intention was to create a part commanding enough to secure the services of Richard Estcourt as Kite, and I am delighted that he proved such a success in the role. I was particularly struck to read that Estcourt 'every night . . . entertained the audience with a variety of little catches and flights of humour.' Jim Broadbent, who is to give us his Kite in this production, is very likely to do the same. He is also a noted comic actor.

I like rehearsal on Saturday mornings. It's a different rhythm. There's only a couple of actors called and three hours' work. One scene to work on, and the weekend in sight. Once you get into the rhythm of rehearsal, weekends are like rafts dotted across the endless ocean. You haul yourself up, get your breath back and look around before plunging on. Just called Jim and Mark this morning and we begin to edit the Fortune-Telling scene. In fact, what we've done is merge the Blacksmith and the Butcher scenes and allocated them to Mark in the character of Pluck the Butcher.

We've mostly used the Butcher's scene, which seems the stronger of the two, but have included the stuff about the signs 'Leo, Sagittarius, Forceps, Furnes, Dixmude, Namur' from the Smith scene. It's a good joke and we don't wish to miss any of the laughs. I bet none of the critics spot what we've done. Mark has a curious hybrid accent at the moment; it's an uneasy marriage between Wales and Ireland, but I'm sure he'll sort that out. Jim is terrific, and very authoritative. He has a great reservoir of stillness. Largely untapped, I think. The less he does, the more sinister he becomes. We've opted not to go for a German accent, but Kite changes slightly for each punter he sees. He's brusque and rather commanding with Pluck, leering and camp with Lucy and Melinda, but rather offhand and businesslike with Brazen. It's clear he doesn't have much time for women, any more than Plume does. Melinda suspects as much: 'Do you think that because I'm a woman I'm to be fooled out of my reason or frighted out of my senses.' He's a nasty piece of work all right. We assess how much he makes from each customer, in modern money, during the Fortune-Telling scene. It's not nothing: £7.50 from Pluck (who twice gives him half-a-crown), Melinda empties her purse, so he probably gets about £30 from her . . . 10s from the parsimonious Brazen ('I must give') and probably a cheque for £1,000 from Worthy once the marriage to millionairess Melinda has been sorted out. There's also the hundred guineas Pluck's mother seems likely to give for her son's discharge. Unlike the Recruiting Scene, where it's possible to sympathize with Appletree and Pearmain, here you direct us to admire Kite's clever villainy. The audience are his confidantes right from the start: 'What, my old friend Pluck the Butcher . . .' he tells them, '. . . I offered the surly bulldog five guineas this morning and he refused it.'

Some versions of the script cut Worthy and Plume hiding under the table in Kite's seance scene. The footnote in our text says that Archer found it 'an extravagantly farcical passage which was doubtless found ineffective and therefore omitted'. But Jim and Linda both think it has great comic potential. I think they have in mind a few 'little catches and flights of humour' of their own. But all this can go too far, George. Robert Hume, the scholar we met in the Theatre Museum, has written a fascinating history on comic biz potential in your plays. Basically, he states, and I agree here, that your plays can be produced either as jolly, sexy romps or as precise and well-observed social comedies. No prizes for guessing which route I would take. Hume takes one part, Squire Sullen from *The Beaux' Stratagem*, and, by tracing the actors who played it in the eighteenth century, concludes that Sullen *became* a comic role played for laughs by the clown in the company. If this was the case, much was lost. Originally, the role would have been given to a serious character actor, the Claudius or Kite figure. Indeed, in your first production, it was taken by Mr Verbruggen, who had played the original Mirabell in *The Way of the World* seven years earlier. This supports what I was saying to you a few days ago

81

about comedy inevitably becoming coarser as theatres grew larger.

On the other hand, we're finding it hard to get a line on Brazen at all – comic or otherwise. He's a puzzling character. Olivier started with a nose and full-bottomed wig in Bill Gaskill's production and stole the show. Is Brazen a complete coward? Ron thinks he might be. On the other hand, John Ross, who wrote the introduction to the Mermaid text, writes 'He doesn't lack a kind of wit. Nor vitally, does he lack courage, but fights Plume briefly, and trumps Worthy's belligerence with the perfectly terrifying proposal to fight a pistol duel with both men standing on a cloak.' This could well be bollocks and a complete misunderstanding of your intentions. He challenges Plume only when it's clear Plume hasn't served abroad (i.e. had battlefield experience) and, although we haven't got to the scene yet, the proposal to fight on a cloak could well be a desperate last attempt to halt the maddened Worthy. Brazen does everything he can to fight with swords, where his own experience and expertise would have been decisive. But perhaps the truth lies between the two? Brazen appears eager for a fight only when he's pretty convinced that the odds are in his favour. But this seems sensible enough behaviour. It's easy for us to take swords on stage for granted. You see them in every production of every classic; somehow they don't have much potency but every English gent carried a lethal weapon at his thigh and had some knowledge of how to use it. It was a subject of much manly interest: 'Pray what did it cost?' Plume can't help enquiring once Brazen has flashed his sword. Silvia, as Jack Wilful the rake, had to acquire an immediate expertise, but then she's always been good at games ('I can do everything with my father but drink and shoot flying.') You would find two things immediately strange about the twentieth century, George. One is that men wear their own hair and, secondly, that nobody goes about armed. To an Englishman, it's always an alarming sight to see a New York cop with a gun at his hip, while in your day there was potential for any scuffle or brawl to end in death. The last ghost of the chivalric code meant that killing was a high-status activity, as long as it was practised between social equals. Nor was the artistic world unvisited by this violence: Byron challenged Southey to a duel, and Sheridan duelled and drew blood over Miss Linley in 1772. A curious sidelight is that you yourself were involved in an accident in Dublin, when you nearly killed a fellow-actor in a stage duel. We're told that this is why you gave up the stage. Perhaps the most famous backstage quarrel was between Charles Macklin and Thomas Hallam in the Green Room at Drury Lane in 1735 over a prop wig. Macklin pierced Hallam through the eye and he subsequently died. Macklin was branded on the hand with a cold iron. All pretty dangerous stuff and enough to make Brazen circumspect without necessarily being an outrageous coward.

## Monday 20 June

### Start of Third Week's Rehearsal

### Dear George,

We went to Shrewsbury today. Caught the 7.40 a.m. from Euston. Jude missed the train. Bacon rolls. Did the actions on the train with Mossie and Lesley: 'engages' at Watford Junction, 'alerts' through Kings Langley, 'jollies' through Berkhamstead, where Max, my father and all his brothers went to school, 'chides' through Tring station, where my uncle Wren used to bring me to see Stanier Pacifics and Black Fives, 'shames' down through Tring Cutting, one of the wonders of Victorian engineering, and 'comforts' as we parallel the Grand Union Canal, scene of many summer voyages. Here's what we did between Watford Junction and Leighton Buzzard.

**Act V, Scene i**

*An Antechamber [adjoining* SILVIA's *bedroom], with a periwig, hat, and sword upon the table*
*Enter* SILVIA *in her nightcap*

**Silvia wants to reassure Rose; Rose wants to blame Wilful**

Silvia: **Engages audience** – I have rested but indifferently, and I believe my bedfellow was as little pleased; **Alerts audience** – poor Rose! Here she comes –

*Enter* Rose

**Jollies** – Good morrow, my dear, how d'ye this morning!

Rose: **Chides** – Just as I was last night, neither better nor worse for you.

Silvia: **Humours** – What's the matter? Did you not like your bedfellow?

Rose: **Stabs** – I don't know whether I had a bedfellow or not.

Silvia: **Braves** – Did not I lie with you?

84

Rose: **Shames** – No – I wonder you could have the conscience to ruin a poor girl for nothing.

Silvia: **Educates** – I have saved thee from ruin, child; **Comforts** – don't be melancholy; **Bolsters** – I can give you as many fine things as the captain can.

Rose: **Snubs** – But you can't, I'm sure. *Knocking at the door*

Silvia: Odso! My accoutrements – (*Puts on her periwig, hat, and sword*) Who's at the door?

[Constable (*without*)]: Open the door, or we'll break it down.

Silvia: Patience a little – *Opens the door*

I don't want to be picky, George, but do you know you use the same joke twice? Rose says 'I don't know whether I had a bedfellow or not' on her final entrance too. Bit casual, George. I know this is essentially a comic scene, but *why* is the Constable arresting them both? Could someone be done for simple fornication? Did this qualify as lewd criminal behaviour? Has the Constable really misunderstood the contents of his warrant? Either way Silvia/Wilful is in trouble having supposedly debauched Rose. We speculate on what went on the night before . . . probably Wilful has supplied enough liquor to get everybody confused and arranges some sort of impromptu marriage service to satisfy Bullock and quieten Rose. They're probably all a bit hung over. We finish the scene by Birmingham New Street. At Wolverhampton our Class 86 Electric is taken off and replaced with an old Bush 47 for the final leg to Shrewsbury.

It seems a backwater, a strange market hill town built on a bend in the river. The bridge into the town is called English Bridge and the bridge out on the other side, to the West, is Welsh Bridge. It's still a border town. Funny accents. Some distinctly Welsh, some very Birmingham and quite a lot of the English county bray, that I'm sure you would remember. Mark's accent for Pluck suddenly appears absolutely accurate and extremely well researched. Because it's hemmed in by the river, the town hasn't grown much. In fact, the Victorian station is built on a large bridge slung across the river, because there's no room for it anywhere else. The town is dominated by Shrewsbury Castle, which has now been turned into a military museum. We went there first. Lesley and Mossie claimed to

85

have found the site of Plume's secret rendezvous with Molly. It was an old gardener's hut. We saw the uniforms which were very vivid and charismatic. The Shropshire Light Infantry had most of their campaign experience in India. Very Kipling. Very Brecht. On the grass in the Castle Yard we get a lecture from Mr Parfitt, the custodian. It seems uniforms hadn't necessarily been invented at the time you came to Shrewsbury. Still, I think we're likely to stretch a point here. We asked eagerly for The Raven, the coaching inn where you staged and wrote the first draft, and where Kite sets up the drinks in the first scene. Mr Parfitt looked shifty. 'I'm afraid you've just missed it,' he said. 'It was knocked down sixteen years ago to make a Woolworths.' All Salopians speak of its passing with some degree of shame. Ironically, Woolworths is itself to be knocked down soon to make way for the Charles Darwin Hypermarket. It turns out you're not Shrewsbury's most famous son after all, George. In fact, I'm sorry to say, that in all the town guides we picked up you're only mentioned once. The Market Square, where you set both recruiting scenes, is recognizable enough and the fine riverside walks with their beeches and elms would probably be as you remember them, and as they were when Melinda stalked Worthy and Brazen duelled with Plume.

I suppose most important is the feeling of a tight, smug little market town, very English, rather friendly, gone a bit Benetton and rather pleased with itself. It's attractive, but not so pretty that it's on the tourist circuit. We were taken round Rowley House, a fine old merchant's town mansion, by Vivien Bellamy, the curator of the Shrewsbury Museum Service. She and her husband, Noel Gaspar, showed us Clive of India's house too. Clive was the local MP for a while, although he never lived in Shrewsbury much. We rehearsed the Recruiting Scene in the Market Square. You can still see the two church clocks Kite orders poor Costar and Tummas to stand guard over. St Chads fell down in a storm in 1788, but the tower is still standing and there was an exhibition of local paintings that Alphonsia Emmanuel and I went to look at – largely rather colourful local landscapes. In the little park, where St Chad's used to stand, two girls were having an early lunch and eating their sandwiches.

There are two streets of very nice town houses hard by St Chads. Apparently, Shrewsbury was big enough to have its own season, but so small that everybody must have known each other intimately and been aware of their business. Some questions we've been asking about the play are answered immediately. How well would Silvia have known Worthy? Very well indeed. How big is the scandal about Molly? Pretty mega. How easily could Melinda avoid Worthy? With difficulty. How much has Shrewsbury been concerned about the romance between Plume and Silvia? They haven't talked about anything else all summer. In fact, I'm surprised they're not talking *still*. The headline in the local newspaper was 'Shrewsbury Men May Have Been Involved in Truck Crash'! We found Melinda's apartment, Worthy's rather substantial town house and the even bigger mansion Melinda has her eye on, now that she's inherited the £1.2 million.

But the biggest triumph was Justice Balance's town house. I'm sure you will remember it. Just outside the castle walls, within a stone's throw of The Raven, is Council House Close. This name has rather confusing associations for us, but you will remember that it referred to The Council of the Welsh Marches. In this little square are two exquisite Queen Anne town houses, with a brick façade built over the wattle-and-daub of much earlier houses. They were completed in 1707 so I like to think they were quite a talking point when you were in town. They give a very clear idea of perfect balance and scale (to borrow the harmonious names of your justices for a moment, George). Vivien Bellamy had arranged for Dr Dudley Ireland, the kindly owner, to show us round. He was a retired GP, and his house was a wonder. The rooms were sizeable but not imposing, with dark oak panelling extending up to the ceilings. The dining room had a cupboard concealed in the panelling for the potty that the gents could use when the ladies had withdrawn. I immediately remembered a passage from Roy Porter: 'Back in the 1660s, Pepys had thought nothing of defecating into a fireplace (servants cleared up the mess) and had himself caught Lady Sandwich "doing sonething upon the pot" in the dining room.' Upstairs, the master bedroom had a beautiful four-poster bed with an immaculate white lace coverlet. The sash windows revealed a sweeping vista down to the Severn with Mrs Ireland at work in the walled vegetable garden. The dressing room to the master bedroom had a double cupboard with a discreet back staircase concealed within it. This permitted the servants to empty the potty while the master and mistress still slumbered. Dr Ireland took us into the terraced garden: a weeping willow looked over delphiniums, stocks, lilies, Canterbury bells and roses. This was the vision of England

that Plume must have yearned for as he sweated through the
dark night before Blenheim. All this and eager Silvia too. No
wonder Plume heads straight back to the therapeutic
harmonies of Shrewsbury. I'd give up my hopes of being a
frigging general all right.

We said goodbye to Dr Ireland and split up with two hours
to kill before our train back. I wandered back through the town
once more; past The Raven (Woolworths) and down Shoemakers' Row. Pride Hill has been turned into a pedestrian centre
and I sat on a bench listening to the different accents. Outside
Boots a lad was fingering his guitar rather hopefully. The med-
ieval street names – Dogpole, Mardall, Shop Latch, Wyle Cot,
Old Fish Street – looked down on the shifting swell of T-
shirted shoppers pushing prams and sucking ice-creams. Down
the hill, I saw Jim and Nick absorbing the local atmosphere and
talking to two girls. They've recognized Jim from his TV series.
They sent Jude off to research the local Army Recruitment
Centre as a punishment for being late. Already I began to re-
cognize faces: the three punks we had seen in the pub at
lunchtime, the two lads working on the hole in the road with
their arses hanging out the back of their jeans that Mossie had
been so struck by. It's a small, small town and the glamorous
eruption of the red-coated, beer-swilling heroes of Blenheim
must have been sensational. There's no way in a place this size
that Silvia could miss Plume or remain unaware of what he's up
to. There must have been real alarm too that Kite and Plume
would disrupt the even balance of the town too much. Act
Five, Scene Two, which we tackle tomorrow, begins with this
debate in progress between Justice Balance and Justice Scale.
Scale is alive to his paternalist responsibilities:

I say 'tis not to be borne, Mr Balance.
This poor girl's father is my tenant, and if I mistake not, her
mother nursed a child for you; shall they debauch our
daughters to our faces?

A complicated network of obligations, relationships and alliances
connected all sections of the community. I think that's why it's
such a wonderful play, George. It moves out of London and,
within the framework and conventions of a comedy, captures
the complex relations of a country town. Critics are unclear
how much your play owes to your time in Shrewsbury. James
writes: '*The Recruiting Officer* really owes more to Farquhar's

experiences in the theatre than it does to his experiences in Shrewsbury . . . It grows out of materials, forms and thoughts that Farquhar worked with all during his career.' I would say that the play's real success is the way it uses the one experience to depict the other.

Caught the train home. Ron, Lesley and David had had to catch an earlier train because they're performing *Greenland* tonight. Poor things. But we're all exhausted and it's only Monday. When we reach King's Cross I haven't the energy or the will to go to the Court; nor can I face the underground. I get a cab to Camden town . . . and so to bed.

## Dear George,

We were all a bit tired today. I was particularly uninspired. Even though our day in Shrewsbury was incredibly useful, I don't refer back to it just yet and feel we must crack on through the text. It was too much fun yesterday and now we must work. We get on to the reconciliation scene between Melinda and Worthy, which I find both funny and moving. It's one of the few short scenes you've written and I sense that it should accelerate the momentum of the play as the second half begins to drive to its conclusion.

Although Worthy and Melinda aren't obviously as glamorous as Plume and Silvia, theirs is a more complex relationship with a longer history. Melinda's journey from disregarded, poor cousin to millionairess is endlessly fascinating. Linda is beginning to play her as a very conventional girl, upset and angry to find herself in such a confusing and unconventional position. Worthy is the kind of part most actors wish to avoid. The very name bespeaks a kind of dullness: he's the dashing hero's worthy best friend. But two things will make Worthy come alive: one is discovering and revealing the real difference between Plume's social position and his own. Plume is an enchanted son, for whom the moral strictures of the community don't apply. However much they may tut, everybody is really ready to wink at the shenanigans with Molly. Worthy is not in the same position: he has already inherited his father's estate and must be very nearly a JP himself. He has more than one foot up the social ladder. He knows how inappropriate are Plume's suggestions for humiliating Melinda in Scene One. He can't possibly 'lie with her chambermaid', or 'hire three or four wenches in the neighbourhood to report that you have got them with child'. The second key is to discover and reveal Worthy's true passion for Melinda. As we work through the scene (Act five, Scene three) we keep going back to the overall intentions and making them more passionate. We start the morning with

'Melinda wants to sort it all out' and 'Worthy wants to punish Melinda', but these are soon discarded and by lunchtime we've got to 'Melinda wants to save Worthy from certain death' and 'Worthy wants to induce Melinda to reveal her true passion.' This beefs the scene up a bit. We go back to the cards again. This time any number red or black indicates the extent of the passion they feel for each other. But, this time, I rig the deck and slip them both tens. The rehearsal room trembles with lambent passion and repressed desire, but we still find it hard to reach the pitch of Melinda's anger with Worthy. She loves him, and she's even prepared to take more than a fair share of the blame herself ('. . . you have been barbarous to me. I have been cruel to you.'). It's always a trap with an argument scene to assume from the start that both parties are going to quarrel, and we try approaching the scene with both trying to play their objectives but to avoid an argument until the moment when they feel they have been unbearably provoked. We make progress.

At lunch, Ron shows me the research he did with Lesley and David on the train back from Shrewsbury last night. They decided what cars each character would drive: Brazen has a Harley-Davidson; Worthy a new Saab or Volvo; Plume a 1975 MGB GT; Melinda a chauffeur-driven Daimler (she previously owned a Morris Minor which she's given to Lucy); Balance a Rover 1000 which he's kept for ten years in immaculate condition; Silvia a Volkswagen Golf convertible that Balance gave her for her twenty-first and Kite doesn't have a car but takes taxis and fiddles the expenses. It's very funny and perceptive, but I rejoice again that we're not doing the modern-dress version.

In the evening, went to see Tony Sher in *The Revenger's Tragedy*. He was terrific. Very witty. Another sex-obsessed play. Tourneur's morality is very convoluted. 'Ope just to one, and then you Ope the Gates to Hell,' Tony advises his sister. I don't think Tourneur is a playwright that you would be very familiar with, George. Augustan audiences favoured comedy and could only take tragedy in rather high-minded doses. The blood-bolted and lustful Jacobeans were thought too raw for eighteenth-century palates and the plays of Tourneur, Webster and Middleton remained unperformed in your time. A pity because I think you would have been struck by their fierce energy.

# 22 June

## Middle of Third Week's Rehearsal: Act V Sc. v

## Dear George,

Became a bit suspicious of the last third of the second half today. It bears all the signs of hurried writing. Too many short scenes. Too many one-line gags, and too many characters suddenly introduced: a constable, a poacher, a collier, two wives, two more justices. Where are they all to come from, George? I love the idea of a scene set in a courtroom but it looks, well, tricky. I don't have enough actors. We reached the point today where Nick Dunning realized he was going to have to go off as Worthy, keep talking in character while changing, and re-emerge immediately as the Constable. I'd rather avoided the subject up to now. He took it very sportingly, I thought, but the stage management aren't taking kindly to the idea of becoming poachers. I'm encountering rather more than passive resistance from the trusty Neil O'Malley. Thank God your stagecraft is so good though, George. It's a relief to direct a play where the author takes proper responsibility for getting characters onstage at the start of a scene and offstage at the end. Nowadays, the influence of films means that writers think they can cut from scene to scene and, all too often, conclude a scene with a stage full of characters and props. The next scene then begins stuffed with fresh impossibilities. Blackouts have done it. They imagine you can do anything in a blackout. Of course, with chandeliers providing a constant light source, you had little option but to provide a realistic means of exit at the end of each scene. But I do appreciate it.

Rehearsed in the theatre for the first time today. It's a wonderful theatre.

Went back over our day in Shrewsbury. Set up various improvisations that gave us all an opportunity to pool our observations. Re-enacted bits of overheard conversations. The improvisations had to last only as long as it took to cross from one side of the stage to the other. Lost children, shopping gossip, people's illnesses. Everybody was struck by how small and intimate the town was, and the impact the recruiting party must have made. We did an exercise called Moral Dilemma. It was focused on Melinda's position the year before the play commenced. Her dilemma is whether to accept £500 per annum and become Worthy's mistress or whether to maintain her virginity and honour. She had to decide. In the play, we never learn what decision Melinda would have made; she asks for a week to consider her position but Lady Richly dies in the meantime. The exercise was partly prompted by the fierceness of the Tourneur play last night and by how hard it is for us now to consider virginity such a precious commodity. We sat in a semi-circle and Linda sat in a chair facing us with her back to the stalls. Turn by turn, we gave her our advice. With no cards to determine their advice on this occasion, the company was very evenly split: some actors spoke from the point of view of their characters. Lesley forcefully led the pro-mistress camp. She should accept the offer and would be a fool to turn it down. It was generous. He was a decent man. Who else was going to come along? Everybody knew she loved him. With £30,000 a year (in present-day money) she could be an inde-pendent woman. Alphonsia, Ron and Jim were much more cautious. Think of the scandal. Everybody would know. A kept woman. Could she remain in Shrewsbury? Would Justice Balance still receive her? Any children she might have would be bas-tards. It would be a decision she would always regret and there would be no going back. How would she feel when Worthy made a suitable match? Did he have somebody in mind already? She would see those children become the legitimate heirs, while hers would always be dependent on charity. Linda then had the right to consult any of us privately. As the exercise went on we all became more agonized. Nick had a last chance to put Worthy's case; but it didn't seem strong enough. Linda then had to walk up the aisle out of the stalls, through the bar at the back, and down the other aisle, having this time alone to think through the position and arrive at a decision. Long-faced and sombre Linda departed. Never was a decision supposedly about pleasure taken with more pain. I thought she wouldn't. The reasons against it were too strong. She came back. We waited silently. She paused. 'I'm going to do it,' she announced. Bed-lam broke out. Nick and Lesley cheering and congratulating her, and the other men shaking their heads. 'I had no choice. I had no choice. What else could I do?' she shouted above the noise. Later we rehearsed the scene again and it's much easier now for Linda to relate to her anger. She's aware of her own weakness. 'Oh, Mr Worthy,' she spits, 'What you owe to me is not to be paid under a seven-year servitude. How did you *use me* the year before, when taking advantage of my innocence and *necessity*, you would have made me your *mistress*, that is, your slave.' The emphasis is temporary but she speaks with venom and self-disgust. A tangible result. We must apply what we learn to the text. It's too easy to have a good time in rehearsal but not show what we've found on stage. This is a note to myself, George.

We do some other improvisations for *Our Country's Good*. We're still trying to find how women behave when their expectations are zero, when they're accustomed to brutality. We try to find the impassive, self-protective toughness that characterizes some of the people in Andrea Dunbar's plays. Lesley and Mossie were in *Shirley* and they do various improvisations of Andrea in rehearsal. Impressively accurate. Linda shows us a local girl coming to join a play her Theatre-in-Education company in Coventry were presenting with local kids. She's sullen, suspicious, silent and withdrawn. She then shows us the same girl coming to rehearsal three weeks later. She's joyful, expectant, skipping into rehearsal. It's very moving. Some of the actors saw a programme on telly last night; it was an American documentary about women who had murdered their husbands. Like the convicts in Australia, they are women who have created an identity out of placing themselves beyond the pale. We re-enact those interviews, but they can't have the depth and richness of the people we've met ourselves because they've already been edited and filtered through somebody else's imagination. It's the sheer unexpectedness and unpredictability of people's behaviour that makes this kind of observation so rewarding and so essential to an actor. This company have great ability to portray what they've seen with accuracy and wit. They're becoming a very impressive group. They take great pleasure from each other, which is good to see. Afterwards, Timberlake puzzled over *Our Country's Good*. She feels she has a lot of scenes but no throughline. Is Ralph's story strong and vibrant enough to bear the whole narrative? Is it different love stories? . . . His Excellency and Arabanoo . . . Duckling and Harry . . . Ralph and Mary. If so, there would be a neat parallel to your plot, George, which is also hinged on different love stories.

# 23rd June

## Third Week's Rehearsal: Act V Sc. vii

### Dear George,

We've been rehearsing your play for nearly three weeks now, mostly round a rehearsal room table, and tomorrow we will begin to move it for the first time. Today I began to lose patience with actions. Of course this was the very moment when we had a particular need of the detail they provide. Without solid groundwork the last scene becomes lost in a miasma of *bonhomie* and blissful resolutions. As you know, the final scenes of comedies always veer in this direction. The scene begins with Balance having risen precipitatedly from the lunch table. This is very neatly and economically suggested with a minimum of props by your stage direction 'with a napkin in his hand, as risen from dinner'. He is outraged that Plume has taken advantage of their friendship and, as it appears, colluded with Silvia in her disguise as Wilful. Balance, playing his cards carefully, reveals that Wilful is an heir and asks for his discharge (a line that invariably raises helpless giggles from David and Mark). Plume asks for the substantial sum of £100 (£6,000 in present-day currency) to release him!

Balance: You shall have it for his father is my intimate friend.

Plume: Then you shall  have him for nothing.

Balance: Nay, sir, you shall have your price.

Plume: Not a penny, sir; I value an obligation to you much above a hundred pound.

Balance: Perhaps, sir, you shan't repent your generosity.

This is the first moment that Balance recognizes Plume as a prospective son-in-law. Balance is staggered that Plume has turned down a year's salary and sharply revises his opinion of him. We rehearsed this scene fairly carefully but kind of trundled over this moment without noticing it. The scene sounded generalized and non-specific. What was at stake seemed unclear. Why was Balance's long-established resistance to the marriage so easily overcome? Back to analysis and actions which we had so far rather skimped. Plume's objective for the scene is probably to enjoy his lunch and keep his star recruit, but when this comes into conflict with Balance's mighty superobjective ('to secure his estate'), Plume finds a graceful way of backing down. This in turn moves Balance to reward Plume with the highest gift he has, Silvia. He is also impressed by Silvia's ingenuity. He has always known 'the extravagance of her passion' but hasn't reckoned on the inventive lengths to which she is prepared to go. Now we're clear that Balance is running or energizing the scene, and it goes much better.

I realized with a shock that this is the first play I've directed in years with a happy ending. We're a bit unused to happy endings in modern drama, George. They went out with the Sixties. Nowadays we usually end plays on a melancholic note of elegant despair. It suits the political climate. Don't misunderstand me, I remember happy endings with affection. Trevor Nunn, an excellent director in an earlier time, struck the note exactly with his productions of Shakespeare's comedies in the early Seventies, which hit an upbeat optimistic note in the final scene, usually ending with music and dancing that invited the audience to celebrate with the actors. RSC curtain calls became legendary for their high-energy charm and salesmanship. *Serious Money* too had an extraordinary, exhilarating song by Ian Dury, but it was at the end of the first half. In New York, Joe Papp spotted the problem immediately: 'You've got the eleven o'clock number at nine o'clock', he said. Broadway audiences want to go out humming the tune whether it's a musical or not. But even in your time, George, the marriages at the end of a comedy were something of a tired convention.

Still, none of this helps the present problem, which is how to make these conventions seem fresh. Part of the trouble, George, is that the scene is underwritten. For example, the excuse you provide for Silvia's eruption into the Balance house is fascinating:

> I think, Captain, you might have used me better, than to leave me yonder among your swearing, drunken crew.

A cocooned life on the capacious Balance estate has not prepared her for the sordid reality of close encounters with the semi-criminal recruits. But there is no follow-through to this intriguing line of thought. Part of the solution must lie with Silvia's real expectation of punishment at her father's hand ('I expect no pardon') and part is her embarrassment that Plume, who has hitherto avoided marriage, may turn her down in public. Unfortunately, you haven't supported this with the text, apart from Silvia's anxious entreaty, 'I have gone too far to make it a jest, sir'. I think we need a few more lines, George. In their absence, we have to emphasize the weight and gravity with which Balance gives away the bride. The actions we chose for Balance's speech are probably over-serious, but they serve to prevent the scene sliding into sentiment before its time. His objective for the unit is to make the marriage work:

Balance: **Prepares Silvia** – No, no Child, your crime shall be your punishment; **surprises Plume** – here, Captain, I deliver her over to the conjugal power for her chastisement; **instructs Plume** – since she will be a wife, be you a husband/a very husband; **confronts Plume binds both** – when she tells you of her love, upbraid her with her folly; **impresses Plume** – be modishly ungrateful; **teaches Plume** – because she has been unfashionably kind; **teases Silvia** – and use her worse than you would anybody else; **grips Plume** – because you can't use her; **moves Plume** – as well as she deserves.

It's probably impossible to play so many actions in one speech but the effort makes Mark glow with serious intent. The last moments of the scene provide the only occasion in the play when Brazen and Bullock are onstage simultaneously, which is difficult, given that both are played by Ron. We opt for Brazen.

## Dear George,

We began to move the play onstage today and
the air was thick with the sound of fragmenting bottle. The
emotional reality and our hard-won perceptions of social
behaviour went right out of the window. Our downfall began
when David Haig as Plume entered wearing a tricorn hat; the
silliness of the whole enterprise became immediately apparent
to us all. Ron Cook was not slow to point out his similarity to
Dick Whittington. The act of bringing your world closer to
ours, George, or the intention of sliding one level of realities
behind the other to provide a perspective was banjaxed.
Sergeant Kite became a jolly rogue and Captain Plume a dashing rake. It looked like anybody's production of any Restoration Comedy. We went back to the actions, we went back to
paraphrasing the script in our own words, in an attempt to claw
back some reality, and began to re-work the text: questioning
some actions and re-emphasizing others. Now we were moving
the play, I realized we had little idea of how Kite and Plume
would greet each other, or how Worthy and Plume would
meet. Would they salute? Would they kiss? Would they bow?
What were the signals for respect or for affection? Having
uncovered the intentions of the characters with the actions,
there's an inclination to plonk these over, rather than work
them through the text.

And what are the characters doing? Only in the Fortune-
Telling scene do you give any indication of onstage activity.
The expository nature of the first scene is a bit naked. They
can't just talk at each other. David and I are keen to establish
Plume's arrival and since the first lines you give him are about
his hard drive up the M5 ('120 miles in 30 hours is pretty smart
riding') we decide to have him wash and even change his shirt
or re-powder his wig before entering town. We've got a village
pump as the centrepiece of the set. It provides a versatile piece
of furniture to be sat on or leaned against. Or even, as perhaps

on this occasion, to pump water from. For the interior scenes a flat flies between the bench at the front and the pump itself. Peter Hartwell has found Rowlandson cartoons featuring different pumps. We focus on the regimental business in Plume and Kite's conversation. Plume needs to be briefed. How many recruits? How stands the country affected? And, above all, 'Were the people pleased with the news of my coming to town?' Plume gets on with his toilet. He's only drawn to sit beside Kite once he hears the alarming news about Molly. The scene with Worthy is easier. We focus on their jolly boyish talk and the sexist nature of their discussion about Silvia and Melinda. It seems all right for them to touch – peer group male bonding. We're less sure about Kite and Plume. We give Plume and Worthy Christian names to make the scene more immediate, and they become Dick Plume and William Worthy. Gradually the two scenes begin to reacquire some of their detail and my nerves begin to settle.

It's easy for the audience to take the characters at their own assessment of themselves, George. You've given Plume's famous speech with its self-insight later in the play when he tells the disguised Silvia, 'I'm not that rake that the world imagines. I have got an air of freedom which people mistake for lewdness.' How will we be able to show the audience that in this first scene? There's some evidence but it's hard to bring out. At first, Plume discusses his affair with Silvia simply in terms of her sexual availability. In fact, both Melinda and Silvia are discussed as sex objects. (Writers have to be careful of that these days, George.) '. . . She would have the wedding before the consummation and I was for consummation before the wedding. We could not agree', boasts Dick Plume. But, as soon as William Worthy indicates that there's been some gossip on this very point, Plume takes offence: '. . . if your town has a dishonourable thought of Silvia it deserves to be burnt to the ground.' In an unguarded moment he tells Worthy that he loves Silvia but corrects himself immediately: 'I admire her frank, generous disposition.' Peer group approval is given to lusting after girls, but not to loving them and certainly not to marrying them.

But the work today provokes thoughts about the scenes to come. By metropolitan standards Plume may not be so gay a blade. It could only be in Shrewsbury that he cuts such a dash. He may even be a bit seedy; perhaps grubby underwear visible as he washes in the first scene. Certainly he and Kite appear like a couple of petty villains. They look a bit like Terry and Arthur, and the old MGB wouldn't have much pulling power in Chelsea with richer, better mounted officers around. The audience must be pointed in this direction because the drift of the play will be that, because he's the hero, he's automatically a suitable match for Silvia. We have to redress the balance and point to his unsuitability as well.

So, before she becomes an heiress what's to stop Plume marrying Silvia? Clearly he fancies her. She adores him and is determined to marry him ('I'll take care he shan't go without a companion'), and she's bludgeoned Balance into giving his reluctant approval. Plume's ambitions as a career officer are the stated obstacle between him and marriage ('Were I once a General, I would marry her'). But Worthy, who has doubtless had Silvia rabbiting away to him more than once, is aware of her determination and passion ('Were you but a Corporal, she would marry you'). Plume's military ambitions must be taken seriously, but perhaps he also has a real sense of unworthiness and immaturity that prevents him pursuing Silvia with the single-mindedness that Archer or Aimwell would have shown in *The Beaux' Stratagem*. Is there a real reluctance to give up batchelor life? Or does he really feel he would be unable to support Silvia? She may not have a huge dowry ('She has fifteen hundred pound in her pocket') but it's fifteen years at a captain's salary.

We do Plume's interview with Silvia again tomorrow (Act Two, Scene One). How would it end if it wasn't interrupted? Would he have proposed? Silvia promises sexual bliss ('. . . you shall die at my feet, or where you will'), but only as long as marriage precedes it ('There is a certain will and testament to be made before hand'). Her overall intention for the scene must be to get Plume to propose. What is Plume's? He might have proposed if the servant hadn't come in, but more likely he wouldn't. He evades the issue by showing Silvia his will made on the battlefield of Blenheim, as evidence of the depth of his feelings, but there's every sign of a return to the impasse of the previous Christmas. His objective still seems to be to persuade her to sleep with him. She won't sleep with him and he won't propose. Does this mean that, even though the action of the play only covers a few days, Plume moves through some rite of passage whereby he stops being one of the lads and by Act Five is ready for marriage and the social responsibilities that will come with the assumption of a great estate? Let's give it a shot.

As for Silvia, I begin to find the Brecht view of the schoolgirl with the crush more and more attractive. She's been spoilt rotten by a doting Balance ('Have I ever denied you anything you asked of me'), and her crush on Plume has been turned into an obsession by his absence and by his patriotic and glamorous exploits. Also there's sex. Both Silvia and Melinda are dying for it: '. . . You are tired of an appendix to our sex, that you can't so handsomely get rid of in petticoats as if you were in breeches,' says Melinda cattily. She's referring to virginity, but both girls know marriage must come first.

P.S. It's nearly 2.30 a.m. and I must go to bed, but I had to write this down to clarify it. We achieved little of it today. I'm writing because we weren't able to do it. But at least we're on our feet now.

# Saturday 25 June
## End of Third Week's Rehearsal: Act I Sc. ii

*Dear George,*

Got a bit stuck with Melinda and Silvia's first meeting again this morning. Partly because it's unclear who is running this scene and partly because we fell into the old trap of assuming that, because it was a quarrel, there must be a history of some antipathy between Melinda and Silvia. Why should there be? Silvia's intention is to renew her friendship with Melinda, whom she hasn't seen all summer ('I envied you your retreat in the country', says Melinda), and also to enlist Melinda's support in the plans she has for Plume. The trouble is that it takes some time to unfold, and instead we get tedious jokes about how full of affectation and pretension Melinda has become now she's got the loot. Frankly, George, I could do without it. The excitement Silvia feels at Plume's arrival, her determination to involve Melinda, and Melinda's irritation that the boorish Plume will now distract Worthy's attention at a vital moment in her campaign to punish/woo him are surely what should be at the heart of the scene, and would provoke a quarrel between the ladies even more effectively than it does at present. It would be great to have a re-write here. Some passages are wonderful: Silvia's description of her life in the country, for example. I'm simply wishing for a re-edit of the existing material.

The manner in which characters greet each other is enormously revealing. I'm not convinced that our social observation in this department has been very detailed: yesterday showed our ignorance. Nick and Mark are our experts in eighteenth-century bowing, but again credibility disappears the moment this period camporama begins. The trouble is that our only cultural reference point is other productions of Restoration plays. So we started the afternoon by just meeting and greeting: in the first place as ourselves – Ron meeting Jim on the first day of rehearsal (very affectionate); Nick meeting his father at his retirement party last week (emotional but formal); David imagining meeting his father when he comes back from holiday (warm but reserved); David meeting his father-in-law (hand outstretched bodies held very distant); Mossie meeting her mother (very cuddly); Alphonsia meeting Linda at the library yesterday (affectionate but confused). We moved from this on to meeting some people we didn't know: and then people we had observed in Shrewsbury. The actors' observation was excellent. An immediate network of close and complex signals could be sensed. It was also possible to make some broad general observations:

1. As a group, we were physically quite accessible and free and there was little inhibition on the grounds of sex i.e. women touched women and women touched men, and men touched men equally easily.
2. In improvisations set in the outside world men touched only quite formally.
3. It was possible to show great emotion with the most distant handshake.
4. Our observation was that ultra middle-class and ultra working-class groups tended to be most physically inhibited.

We then moved back 250 years and applied these observations to characters meeting in the play. We discovered an immediate and fierce taboo on middle-class men touching middle-class women (Plume's meeting with Silvia should be a room's width apart). On the other hand, your remarks about men kissing each other in the army led us to middle-class men touching middle-class men with pleasure and delight. Balance and Plume, or Plume and Worthy have physical access to each other in a way that would be quite wrong in a post-Victorian world. Middle-class men's accessibility to peasant girls was free and easy: Plume is able to touch up Rose all he wants, while Rose and Bullock only ever exhibit physical contact by cuffing each other. We worked on Kite's greeting of Plume. We wanted to show considerable emotion but remain physically quite distant. I remembered the scene in *Tumbledown* where the NCO greets the injured Robert Lawrence on his return to the regiment. A quivering depth of emotion was clearly signalled in the salute. We had already learned, from the curator of the Castle Museum in Shrewsbury, that saluting had evolved from raising one's visor to show one was a friend. Homage à Richard Eyre, we discovered we could convey a huge range of emotion by a primitive form of saluting. Gradually we worked out a physical language and Brazen's affected greetings began to stand out. A picture of a society began to emerge where bowing seemed an extension of normal behaviour which could be used to express a range of emotion and approval, as opposed to a series of rather lifeless and unexamined moments.

There are some characters in every play who don't really meet: for example, Silvia and Worthy are barely on stage together, but they have been brought up in the same town, share the same class background and must know each other extremely well. Is it possible to show this closeness in the two or three references they have to each other? We did a simple exercise when one character is placed in the centre of a semi-circle and is approached by the other characters in turn. They must first find something as positive as they can to express about the seated character (e.g. Silvia admires Worthy's loyalty). The task is then to find a line in the text with which to express that: we go for 'He's a gentleman of parts and fortune.' If you also use the same exercise to find as negative a feeling as possible about the seated character, you then begin to widen the range of emotion that governs each relationship. Also, it's a way of discovering the exception. For example, we know that Balance respects Worthy, or that Silvia loves Plume. Is there anything they dislike about each other? Today Plume was in the chair and the exercise helped to define Rose's range of feelings towards the Captain. They moved from adulation to confusion and suspicion, as he begins to be more and more elusive and evade the promises he made her. Worthy discovered both the excitement he has that Plume has returned to Shrewsbury and the mounting resentment he has that his friend's advice on the courting of Melinda is misplaced and possibly disastrous. Balance revealed both his genuine affection for Plume ('I like him the better; I was such another fellow at his age') and his equally valid worry that there was some moral weakness in the boy which had harmful potential ('I'm glad my daughter's gone fairly off though'). Melinda loathed his boorish drunkenness, but had a sneaking admiration for his candour. Silvia, of course, adored him to distraction but, despite her bravery on the sub-ject, couldn't fully suppress an alarm about his constancy and so on. Any group of people, like, for example, the company of us doing the play, have a complex range of semi-expressed and repressed feelings about each other. The tendency when por-traying that same group on stage is to go for direct emotions and simple colours. Sometimes this would be the correct decision: it's of little use exploring the complexities of Rose's relationship with Melinda if there is no opportunity at all to show it on stage. But the real value of the exercise is that it stimulates us to explore the characters' lives beyond the play, and then forces us to bring those discoveries back and apply them to the text.

A dreary morning, but an exciting afternoon.

*Dear George,*

I've decided to cut some of the stuff about Melinda's arriviste pretensions at the beginning of Act One, Scene Two between Silvia and Melinda. It's only to be expected that after 250 years some of your jokes won't have quite the same impact, and I think the laborious puns on 'airs' fall into just such a category. I hope you won't mind too much. I really don't have many other cuts in mind, except for the Fortune-Telling scene, which we have edited for the quite different reason of repetitive dramatic structure. If you were to tell me that Silvia's teasing of Melinda previously provoked great hilarity I would certainly believe you, but, on the other hand, I bet there's always been a problem with the structure of the second half hasn't there? Come on, George, admit it. I quite accept that the Fortune-Telling scenes should provide a bravura set piece for Sergeant Kite but they can't be permitted to do so at the expense of the energy and drive of the whole story. There are problems too with the Courtroom (Act Five, Scene Five) which might be expedited by some judicious cutting. It's not entirely down to not having enough actors. The dramatic purpose of the scene seems unclear, and the style is confused. Finally, there is some under writing at the very beginning of the play in Sergeant Kite's Recruiting scene, but we're going to have another go at that on Monday and I'll write to you then.

What would help is if we could clarify the time-scale. Sometimes you're very specific about the time of day and at others it seems vague. For example, we know that Plume arrives in Shrewsbury at four in the afternoon, having ridden for thirty hours. So he started off at ten the previous morning; but it's much less clear what the time is, say, at the beginning of Act Three. Plume and Worthy are talking in the Market Place, and Rose is selling chickens, but is it the next morning or the next afternoon, or the day after? If we could fix this, it would go some way in helping to determine what the characters might be doing at any given point.

106

We've already established that the play takes place over a few days in mid-September: here's a possible time-frame: the events that verifiably happen in the play are in italics, the rest is inspired speculation.

| | |
|---|---|
| Sat 13 Aug: | Plume and Kite at Blenheim |
| Sat 10 Sep: | Orrery's regiment set sail from Ostend |
| Mon 12 Sep: | Plume and Kite back in London: Kite continues straight on to Shrewsbury, while Plume stays at the Rose Tavern, Russell Street, on regimental business. |
| Wed 14 Sep: | Kite arrives in Shrewsbury |
| Mon 19 Sep: | After a final weekend in London (not on regimental business) Plume sets off. Stays night at Lygon Arms, Broadway. No bill presented to hero of Blenheim. |

| | | |
|---|---|---|
| *Tue 20 Sep:* | 6 am | Plume rides off towards Worcester and Shrewsbury. |
| | 9 am | Balance and Silvia leave in the coach and four from Balance Hall, Aston Balance, Salop. |
| | 12 noon | They arrive in Shrewsbury. Balance sees Kite and learns Plume is en route. |
| | *2 pm* | *Kite recruits in the Market Square (I.i).* |
| | *4 pm* | *Plume arrives to meet Kite and Worthy (I i).* |
| | *4.30 pm* | *Silvia takes tea with Melinda (I ii).* |
| | 5 pm | Plume checks into the Raven. (Broaches the Barcelona at Horton's.) |
| | *6 pm* | *Calls on Balance for a drink and to meet Silvia (II i). News of Owen's death . . .* |
| | *7 pm* | *. . . arrives by the Evening mail and Silvia is ordered back to the country (II ii).* |
| | 8 pm | Plume dines at the Raven and during the evening he and Kite meet intermittently at The Lion, The Prince Rupert and The Bear and Ragged Staff doing their |

107

|          |             | recruiting double act. |
|----------|-------------|------------------------|
|          | 10 pm       | Silvia arrives back at Balance Hall. Servants don't expect her. No supper. Furious. |
|          | *12 midnight* | *Kite lures Costar and Thomas into the Market Square (II ii). They are recruited.* |
| *Wed 21 Sep:* | 2 am   | Kite drinks with Plume back at the Raven. Plume very drunk. |
| *Wed 21 Sep:* | 4 am   | Bullock and Rose arrive with produce in Market Square. |
|          | *9 am*      | *Worthy calls on Plume for pre-breakfast drink (III i). Plume very hung over. Rose and Bullock are on their . . .* |
|          | *10 am*     | *. . . way home. They meet Plume. Plume takes Rose to the Raven.* |
|          | 10.30 am    | Silvia slips away from Aston Balance. She can stand it no longer. She nicks Owen's suit. |
|          | *12 noon*   | *Melinda and Lucy meet Brazen (III ii). Worthy enlists Plume who has been drinking all morning to* |
|          | *12.30 pm*  | *bait Brazen and they meet Silvia disguised as Wilful. Brazen and Plume duel.* |

*Interval*

|          | *2 pm*      | *Rose finds Bullock (IV i). Plume sobers up a bit and talks to Wilful/Silvia.* |
|----------|-------------|------------------------|
|          | 2.30 pm     | Kite opens his booth as the Fortune-Teller. His first customer is Melinda, who . . . |
|          | *3 pm*      | *. . . unburdens her secret to Lucy (IV i).* |
|          | *4 pm*      | *Kite has already recruited a tailor and a shoemaker. He's visited again by Melinda . . .* |
|          | *4.30 pm*   | *. . . and by Brazen (IV ii).* |
|          | 9 pm        | Kite, Plume and Worthy have a bachelor evening at the Raven. Maybe Plume . . . |

| | |
|---|---|
| 12 midnight | . . . pays a secret visit to Molly, but . . . |
| 1 am | . . . Wilful is entertaining Rose and Bullock, who daren't go home. At Bullock's . . . |
| 1.30 am | . . . insistence they go through some sort of cod wedding ceremony. Bullock exhausted . . . |
| 2 am | . . . he's been up for nearly twenty-four hours. Rose expectant. . . . *and then sadly disappointed by Wilful's performance.* |

| | | |
|---|---|---|
| *Thurs 22 Sep:* | *7 am* | *Dawn raid by Constable (V i) arrests Bullock, Wilful and Rose and brings them . . .* |
| | *9 am* | *. . . to a preliminary hearing (V ii) before Balance and Scale.* |
| | 9 30 am | Having missed Silvia the night before, servants set out from Aston Balance on foot. |
| | *10 am* | *Worthy is prompt for his appointment with Melinda (V iii).* |
| | *11 am* | *Plume meets Brazen (V iv) who reveals his rendezvous with Melinda.* |
| | *11.30 am* | *The Court sits (V v) and, at the same time, Brazen and Worthy nearly fight (V vi).* |
| | *1 pm* | *Balance sits down for lunch (V vii) but is interrupted by the arrival . . .* |
| | *1.30 pm* | *. . . of the servant from Aston Balance.* |
| | *2 pm* | *All is resolved.* |
| | 9 pm | The marriages can't be arranged for at least two weeks so no doubt Plume . . . |
| | 12 midnight | . . . joined by Worthy and Balance, have another night in the Raven. While Melinda buys Silvia dinner at The Prince Rupert . . . |
| | 1 am | . . . and Kite drinks alone and torments Costar and Tummas. |

It's a fairly action-packed three days all right but I reckon it makes sense. The one occasion credibility is pressured is when Lucy refers to Worthy being 'taken up' with Plume 'these two days'. He's barely been in town twenty-four hours by our reckoning but at least they're spread over two days. On the off-chance, I rang Shrewsbury Police Station to ask when the Shrewsbury Magistrates Court sat. Wednesdays and Thursdays was the answer! This is, of course, quite perfect. Balance arrives in town on Tuesday for the Wednesday and Thursday first session of the autumn term.

# Monday 27 June
## Start of Fourth Week's Rehearsal Act I Sc. i

## Dear George,

I had originally thought that we might begin the play with Sergeant Kite's famous recruiting speech either set outside on the steps of the Royal Court or in the foyer itself. My production of *The Speakers* for Joint Stock, with Bill Gaskill, had pioneered what is now known as promenade theatre. *Road* had been a triumph in Sloane Square in Simon Curtis's promenade production a few years earlier. I was anxious to taste these triumphs again, and confident that the street theatre nature of Kite's speech could be exuberantly caught in the same way. But both Ron and Jim were chock-full of lack of enthusiasm. They were veterans of these occasions: Jim with Ken Campbell and The National Theatre of Brent, and Ron at Stratford in *The Dillon*. They were both convinced the audience's attention would be dissipated. They would become confused, and it would become harder to refocus and restart the play with Plume's entrance. Ron rehearsed the embarrassing moments that would occur with acquaintances in the audience at tedious length. But the trouble isn't resolved by restoring the play to the stage. With David poised for his entrance as Plume, Lesley bewigged and becorseted in the wings, Jim appearing as Kite, and Jude having rehearsed his drumming for hours on end at the Royal Military School of Music, we would be down to a mob of six assorted Salopian townspersons. It would appear that Shrewsbury had received a visitation from The Black Death rather than the Grenadiers. Could we do without a mob altogether and Kite play the speech directly to the audience? In fact, we tried this in an earlier rehearsal and it seemed understandably flat; but then again, George, the lines you've provided for the mob appear a bit sporadic and tentative. Since our mob were likely to be at least 50 per cent female should some lines be provided for them? Or should Linda appear in her guise as Tummas Appletree? Also, if this feeble mob *were* on stage, how could they disappear so swiftly at Plume's entrance?

111

In fact, I had been cooking up some possible solution to this since the rehearsal ten days ago, which had so set me back. You must understand that, after your death, *The Recruiting Officer* became, quite simply, the most popular play of the century, with 164 performances in the 20 years following. This far outstripped your nearest rival, *Hamlet*, with a mere 135 in the same period. Several writers attempted to emulate your success: among these was Isaac Bickerstaffe, also a fellow Irishman. He seems to have been a sort of literary manager on Garrick's staff at Drury Lane. In this capacity, he adapted Wycherley's *The Plain Dealer*, as well as enjoying considerable success with his own ballad operas: *Love in a Village, The Padlock* and *Thomas and Sally*. He also wrote one called *The Recruiting Sergeant!* Well, George, of course it's a sentimental and indifferent old boiler that hasn't endured. There's no doubt it's simply a blatant piece of genial opportunism on Isaac's part, but it occurs to me that, as you're unable to undertake any re-writing of the first scene, why don't I simply draft in a few lines from *The Recruiting Sergeant*. I honestly don't think your man, Bickerstaffe, would mind a jot. He gave great encouragement to Oliver Goldsmith, whose plot for *She Stoops to Conquer* is recognizably borrowed from Bickerstaffe's own *Love in a Village*. He, in turn, had nicked it from Marivaux's *Le Jeu de l'Amour et du Hasard*. Bickerstaffe even helped Goldsmith in rehearsals, but wasn't around for the first night. It appears that his fondness for guardsmen led to blackmail and he departed swiftly for a holiday on the Continent. A less tolerant age, George, to which we are fast returning.

There's some dialogue Bickerstaffe uses in the lyrics of a song, between the Recruiting Sergeant and a protesting mother in the crowd, that could be pressed into service; they can be spoken as between Thomas Appletree and his mother: they are arguing over the Sergeant's grenadier cap:

Thomas: Let me see it.

Mrs A: Come away Thomas.

Thomas: Let me try it.

Kite: Ay, let him see if it becomes him. He is tall enough to be a great man.

Mrs A: Let it alone I tell thee, Tummas. Men by him are hocus-pocust into danger and fatigue.

*Backstage: The photo is timeless. Only the plastic cups give it away.*
*L to R: Jude Akuwudike, Linda Bassett, Jim Broadbent, Nick Dunning*
*and Alphonsia Emmanuel. Warsaw. Nov. 1988.*

*Lesley Sharp on the steps of the Royal Court.*

*Lesley Sharp as Silvia Balance.*

*Mossie Smith as Rose.*

*Lesley and Mossie.*

*Sergeant Kite studying the movement of the stock exchange
in his dressing room.*

*Alphonsia Emmanuel and Linda Bassett as Lucy and Melinda.*

*Nick Dunning and Mark Lambert as Worthy and Justice Balance.*

*Ron Cook as Captain Brazen. Shrewsbury in the background.*

*A break in* Our Country's Good *rehearsals.*
*Timberlake is looking surprinsingly relaxed or maybe she's just exhausted.*

Our Country's Good. *Visiting hours.*
*L to R: Lesley Sharp, Alphonsia Emmanuel, Nick Dunning,*
*Jim Broadbent, Ron Cook, Linda Bassett, Jude Akuwudike.*

Kite: Do but let him try the cap of Honor, mistress.

Mob (Nick): Let him try it.

Mrs A: I don't fear thee. Nor the justices in league with you. My son has enough at home. He has his eightpence a day and bread enough. So you let him be.

Thomas: Let me but hold the cap, mother.

Mrs A: Get thee home, Thomas, and a trudging quick.

Thomas: But mother

Mrs A: I'll make thee repent. I'll take a stick to thee.

Kite: Shame mistress, that you range your artillery between him and honour.

Mrs A: Call you this work honour? (exit Mrs A and Thomas)

Kite: Come gentlemen who fears the French after this. Their cuirassiers and bombardiers were sparrows as it were to the wrath of this goodwife of Salop. Who has the cap now? It becomes you mightily, sir. Behold a great man.

. . . and then back to your dialogue.

Well, it's not Shakespeare; it's not Farquhar either, but it's good serviceable Bickerstaffe, and it gives the scene more depth and life. Thomas now appears eager for contact with the glamorous military and his entrance into the recruiting scene is prepared here.

I prompted Jim to start the scene first standing on a crate in the middle of the rehearsal room. The other actors were still on their tea-break and gradually began to listen and focus. The crowd are healthily sceptical. They aren't unfriendly to the hero of so many campaigns, but they do suspect trickery ('Won't the cap list me?'). Jim had been to see men selling watches in Brick Lane on Sunday and, although he can't yet speak fast enough to do what he wants, his inclination and his instinct are marvellous. His action, or main intention, is simply to entertain the crowd, to make friends, reassure them and ask them back to The Raven for a pint. The hard sell will come later. We used the cards once more to determine the receptivity of people's response. Jim spotted the enthusiasts immediately and worked the crowd. In fact, with the new dialogue, our tiny crowdlet have a range of responses from considerable enthusiasm (red eight, Linda) through mild interest (red three, Alphonsia) and curiosity (red two, Ron), to suspicion (black four, Mark), hostility (black five, Nick) to implacable emnity (black ten, Mossie). It immediately gave the scene independence and depth. Most of the time in rehearsal is spent diagnosing the problems. I come to rehearsal with a solution relatively infrequently, but today was one of those occasions and it was gratifying that it worked.

This evening I reflected that Bickerstaffe was right about at least one thing. 'A Recruiting Sergeant's worst friend is the mother', Sergeant James had told us with great feeling .

We didn't take any staging decisions today, but I begin to feel that staging somehow *among* the audience, but not insisting they get involved, may be the answer. Placing it onstage will still reveal our meagre resources. Jude's drumming is becoming a force to be reckoned with. This is another product of our research: after Marlborough's campaigns many regiments had black musicians (especially black drummers) attached to a recruiting party as an element of exotic appeal.

What do you think about Isaac, George? I bet nobody will notice, and, on reflection, I think he will be thrilled if we borrow a small piece of his dialogue. Mossie likes it.

# Tuesday 28th June
## Week Four

## Dear George,

Rather an extraordinary day in rehearsal yesterday. It was largely concerned with Timberlake's play but I think you would find it fascinating nonetheless. Linda and Alphonsia had been to see Rosie, who had been first in Holloway then in Styal. Timberlake had needed detail about how one became a criminal. Some of the women convicts on the First Fleet had been professional thieves and some had stolen through immediate necessity. At what point did necessity become your profession? Linda and Alphonsia were exuberant and excited, but disciplined themselves to say nothing until they had reported back to us. They sat facing a semi-circle of the rest of us and re-enacted their interview. Both of them became Rosie, sometimes replying simultaneously but, above all, prompting each other with the detail. The rest of us became Linda and Alphonsia listening and asking questions. Thus their research was fed to Timberlake. And, on this occasion, it was very successful. Both actresses hit on the same personality: perky, London, sharp and bright, and in the course of the hour-long improvisation came up with an astonishing amount of detail. Like Dabby Bryant, the witch in *The Playmaker*, Rosie originally came from Cornwall. She had a poor, rural background. She had liked school because you got fed. She had started by breaking into the big houses just to look. The first thing she actually stole or rather ate, was part of a green jelly she found in a fridge. We were all aware of the shocking and immediate parallels both to the women in *The Fatal Shore* and to the Mayhew accounts we had read. Rosie spent time in approved school, went to prison, protested, got put in solitary for six months, came out, started doing bank robberies with a gang, got a lot of money, nice house, her girlfriend spent it, went back in prison. Now going straight. The detail was impressive.

There were three key moments in Linda and Alphonsia's

115

perception of her history. The first was her betrayal by her father. Her mother had died and she was up before the Juvenile Court for crimes that in fact her father had put her up to. In court, he put the blame on her: 'She stole money from her mother's purse.' Rosie went wild, kicking, screaming, biting and punching until she was hauled out and restrained. The second was a night in her first prison when she lay awake all night rigid with fear after she had been threatened by a gang of prisoners. She had seen them beating up another prisoner and the screws had found out, but the gang thought she had grassed on them. Through the night, she kept bending a spring from her bed to and fro until it broke. The rest of the night, while it was getting light, she spent sharpening the spring against the concrete wall. Next morning she attacked the toughest of the women as she came through the washroom door. She beat her up and thus gained respect and a position. The final key moment was the account of the months in solitary which nearly broke her spirit. Discovering her own limitations terrified her. She never pushed the authorities that far again. That's what the beatings must have done. Discovering how many you could take. There are terrifying descriptions in *The Fatal Shore* of flesh flayed off the back; but Ralph Clark's offhand descriptions of floggings where the recipient 'ordered to receive a hundred lashes could only bear seventy-three' are less graphic but even more chilling.

The progression from looking hungrily at green jelly in somebody's kitchen to carrying a shot-gun in a highly organized bank-raid was entirely convincing. A good piece in the jigsaw to help Timberlake. Rosie said the best bank robberies were very like putting on a play. They were well-rehearsed, you each had a particular part to play, and the problem with first night nerves was terrible.

It was good to be able to give Timberlake our full focus and a good afternoon's work. As we've concentrated on *The Recruiting Officer* she's been working at home, excluded from our magic circle. I hope she's all right. It seems a reckless act of unreasonable confidence in all our abilities to schedule a play for performance in a major theatre in ten weeks' time, when only three scenes have been written and I haven't yet read a word. Four weeks out and our journey is beginning to resemble the eight-month voyage of the First Fleet. Will we ever get there . . . and what will the country look like?

116

# Wednesday 29th June
## Week Four: Act III Sc. i

*Dear George,*

Bit of a stolid day in rehearsal. Got through a few scenes but it seemed uninspired. In the afternoon we focused on Balance, who is, after all, the apex of society in the play. It's the only Restoration Comedy I can think of that doesn't have at least a baronet at the centre of it. It thus marks a particular stage in the downwardly mobile social progress of English comedy: Shakespeare dealt with kings and dukes, Wycherley and Vanbrugh with baronets, you at least with a Justice of the Peace; and today we put plumbers, vicars and window cleaners at the centre of our comedies.

The only insight I had was when I realized what high status Balance is afforded by the whole community and how embarrassing it is for Worthy when Brazen doesn't know his name and, through an absurd misunderstanding, imagines Balance's name to be Laconic. It's embarrassing for everybody when somebody of such high status is unrecognized. Silvia's reaction and behaviour in the Court scene has great richness to it: she's a spoilt wealthy girl who probably hasn't seen the realities of his corrupt world too closely. Spending time in prison, not to mention spending the night with Rose, and seeing things from a male perspective mark a rite of passage for Silvia too. She experiences the world outside the confines of Aston Balance; and the Court scene could be played to show her in a psychological crisis as she confronts her father for the first time. But is this what you want, George? It seems to turn on the character of Balance, with whom you do seem to want to have it all ways at once. I'm not asking for the Brechtian simplicity of a conniving landowning villain but, at different times, Balance becomes an ideal to be emulated (Plume's last speech), a figure of wisdom and paternal authority (early scenes with Silvia) and a corrupt buffoon (Court scene). How can we reconcile all this? At any rate, Mark must play him with more authority and status – a village Hampden, accustomed to authority.

117

Saw some of the costumes in the evening and they looked like, well, they looked like costumes. Part of the trouble is the associations. Even if people did wear yards of curtain fabric in the eighteenth century, it doesn't evoke the period. It evokes other productions or it evokes curtains. Perhaps Peter and I should have gone for a bolder approach. Could we costume the play by using modern clothes of a similar cut? Or could you combine jeans and a military jacket? Could Balance have a tweed suit underneath a period coat? In Bogdanov's Henry cycle something similar was tried. Here the intention would not be to startle the audience with a new awareness but rather to make what the actors are wearing seem like clothes not costumes. Our other necessity is also to cut costs. If you start breaking costumes down they always look to me like broken-down costumes. How do you get them to look like clothes people are wearing, and have bought with their own budgets and dress-sense? I feel very unfashionable. People want concepts. They think that's what directors do; have concepts. I hate fucking concepts: everybody wearing different shades of lilac to mean they're rich, a shiny fabric to show they're decadent. The budget is going over again too. The extra £5,000 has been swallowed by the wigs alone, and the advance has barely moved from last week. The costumes are now coming from Adrian Noble's production in Bristol eight years ago. I hope he got it right that's all, and I long for the day when he uses *my* hand-me-down costumes for his productions in pissing Stratford.

In the evening, Hartwell glues me back together, and takes me back to the great painters of your period: Rowlandson and Hogarth at one end of the social scale, Reynolds and Gainsborough at the other. He shows me the outline and the cut and how the clothes lead to the behaviour. How society and social behaviour is directed by the costumes and how this is, after all, what we are working towards.

P.S. Later . . . I can't sleep. Later still . . . I still can't sleep. I've taken one valium already. One more and I'll be soggy all morning in rehearsal. Why isn't the advance moving? This is a classic, isn't it? People are supposed to like classics. I need a good day tomorrow.

# Thursday 30th June

## Dear George,

I've made Plume pretty drunk in Act Three, Scene Two. He's been boozing all morning at The Raven, comes on, meets Worthy and has a long piss. 'You an't drunk?' enquires Worthy anxiously (action 'solicits'). 'No, no whimsical only' (action 'entertains') responds Plume. But in fact his pissed state determines the tone of the whole scene with Brazen, and his rather offensive cod courting of Melinda. This confirms Melinda's suspicions of Plume's atrocious behaviour and his appalling influence on Worthy: 'I warrant he has never been sober since that confounded captain came to town.' In fact, there's quite an emphasis on drinking throughout the play. 'I can do everything with my father but drink and shoot flying', regrets Silvia. She doesn't mean she doesn't have the odd glass of sherry or bottle of claret. She means that there's a taboo on women becoming so totally arseholed that they just slide under the table.

What does Roy Porter have to say? He writes on the prodigious consumption of claret. 'To gain a reputation as a blade one had to be at least a three-bottle man. Sheridan, Pitt the Younger and the Greek scholar, Parson, were all reckoned six-bottle men . . . "Drunk as a lord" was a very apt phrase. And they drank competitively. As man-about-town William Hickey put it, "I was always ambitious of sitting out every man at the table when I presided." Hard drinking obeyed no social boundaries. In his youth, Samuel Johnson remembered, "All the decent people in Lichfield got drunk every night, and were not thought the worse of . . .", and, of course, the intoxication of many of the London poor in the Gin Craze was lethal: "Drunk for a penny, dead drunk for tuppence; straw free." ' Lichfield is, of course, where you set *The Beaux' Stratagem*, George, so I'm sure Shrewsbury was just the same. I reckon Balance is at least a three-bottle man, Plume a five-bottler and Kite about an eight-bottle fellow. Indeed, Balance apologises to Worthy for having 'to allow a day or two to the death of my son . . . afterwards I'm yours over a bottle or how you will'. Indeed, he will be.

I must confess that part of the inspiration for these reflections came from Nick and Jim's visit to the Sergeant's Mess in Whitehall Barracks on Tuesday night. Yesterday morning both were pale and thoughtful after seven pints and seven double vodkas each. They had been entertained by our Recruiting Sergeant friend, Sarnt-Major James. It appears the army is still an eighteenth-century haven of serious drinking. As the evening progressed, and it became clear that a glass could not hit the bar without severe danger of an immediate refill, extreme friendliness broke out between the two parties. Tickets for Wimbledon, Lords, the Lord Mayor's Show and The Royal Tournament could be procured with no bother. (It turned out that the Sergeants' Mess managed the security at Wimbledon as a small piece of private initiative.) They firmly believed that the sergeants ran the army for their own benefit. They were wonderfully positioned between the officers and the men. Their opinion of officers wasn't overwhelmingly high ('some of them are all right . . . some of them are prats . . . but they all need looking after'). Beneath the *bonhomie* lurked some fairly ferocious opinions: ('Bullying in the army? No, it doesn't happen. You get some fun sometimes that's all. You heat this iron so the bloke can see it . . . red hot . . . then you make him lie on his front and hold him there . . . and put a cold iron on his back . . . oh ho, they scream. It's a laugh . . . sometimes they even break out in blisters.') Late in the evening, an excerpt from your play was read, George. Jim (very popular because he had been recognized from the TV series) read Kite's opening speech in the Market Place. The Sergeants' Mess loved it. They were also amazed it was written so long ago. It seemed to them just the kind of speech that could well be heard now. So your play passed a very vigorous test of authenticity, George.

It would be possible to take what we did today a stage further and chart progress through the play by what the characters are drinking at any particular time: sherry for Plume's early evening visit to Balance (Act Two, Scene One). That fresh cask of Barcelona at Horton's (mentioned at the end of Act One, Scene One) for the rest of the evening. Finishing with a yard or two of humming ale before the Recruiting Scene (Act Two, Scene Three), where all four protagonists must be well pissed. This could make Kite aggressive, Plume rather imperial and

120

Tummas and Costar confused, tired and emotional. Next day Plume probably starts drinking with Worthy at breakfast time in the Market Place (Act Three, Scene One). A brandy or two to knock the hangover on the head and then March beer at The Raven all morning as he pursues the fatiguing business of recruiting. Maybe Silvia will live to regret her bravery and imprudence. Will Plume give up drinking after they are married? Or in after years will Silvia relate how last night he stumbled into Balance Hall 'at his usual hour of four, wakened me out of a sweet dream of something else, by tumbling the tea table which he broke all to pieces; after his man and he had rolled about the room, like sick passengers in a storm, he comes flounce into bed, dead as a salmon into a fishmonger's basket; his feet as cold as ice, his breath as hot as a furnace, and his hands and face as greasy as his flannel night-cap'.

But, no, George, that's not Plume. You were thinking of someone else. This is Mrs Sullen's description of her husband from your next play, *The Beaux' Stratagem*.

PS  Today was as heady as yesterday was mind-locked.

Friday 1st July

Act III Sc. ii

## Dear George,

I'm glad you couldn't get to rehearsal today,
because I was as about as inspired as an old pudding. I spent
forever staging Silvia's first entrance as Jack Wilful. Part of the
problem is that it is easy for us to spot the comic outline of a
scene, or rather it's particularly easy for such deft comics as Ron
Cook and Jim Broadbent to spot what we have come to call the
CP (Comic Potential). They are as sensitive to hidden caches
of CP as water diviners are to an underground spring. Sometimes, this makes it harder to locate the underlying drives and
intentions that energize the scene in the first place. So, Silvia's
arrival very quickly became a jokey scene about Wilful being
tugged to and fro by Plume and Brazen. We then progressed
slowly to it being a considerably unfunny scene about nothing
much at all, before going back to what we should have done in
the first place and taking the objectives seriously. In this case,
both captains want to enlist Wilful. Why? What is the financial
motive? Is it a particular prize to enlist a gent? Or are Plume's
later words to be taken at face value? ('You must know in the
first place, then, that I hate to have gentlemen in my company
for they are always troublesome and expensive, sometimes
dangerous.') As soon as we found, or even invented, the reasons
why recruiting Wilful is a strong drive for both men, the competition and desire to outwit each other gives a backbone to the
scene from which the CP naturally springs. How one has to
learn the first lessons again and again.

At the beginning of the rehearsal, we had talked of dressing
Lesley up as a boy and getting her into El Vino's or The Garrick
Club. We emphasized how she should look as much like a lad
as possible. One day she smeared her face lightly with vaseline
and experimented with chopped up bits of beard. It looked
very good. But working through rehearsal today I think I realized
that authenticity isn't the point. I should have remembered
those pantos at the Lewisham Hippodrome.

122

Although Linda's *tour de force* as Thomas Appletree may throw them off the scent a bit in this production, the audience *know* Wilful is a girl. They therefore don't require high definition persuasion. Their pleasure is in observing the actress' skills in portraying a man. Then enjoyment is enhanced by their superior knowledge to the characters on stage, and they are delighted and flattered to be treated as the actress' confidante and best friend ('What's here? Rose, my nurse's daughter. I'll go and practice.') And, of course, it always works. Nobody ever finds out. Never once, in any pantomime or play, does another character onstage say: 'Now hang on a minute there's something funny going on here.' Although we must play it as though it were a constant possibility. Lesley is now wonderful in her tentativeness when she first comes on. Anxiously, she keeps the width of the stage away from Plume and hastily extemporizes some responses to questions she hasn't fully thought through. 'What are you, sir?' enquires Brazen. 'A rake', proffers Lesley hopefully, in a deep voice. I have no idea what great wellspring of pleasure is touched by observing women play men or men play women, but it is a pleasure as old as drama. And, I now realize that, in your time too, this pleasure must have gone far deeper than simply seeing the actresses' legs. Burlington Bertie or Jack Wilful or the gender confusion in *Cloud Nine* are great theatrical creations. They demonstrate tangible acting skills but they provoke analysis as well as pleasure because they observe the danger of sexuality without the harmful possibility of reality. You would have enjoyed talking to Bertolt Brecht about this one.

# Saturday 2nd July
## End of Week Four: Act IV Sc. i

## Dear George,

I understand more clearly every day why Brecht was so keen to do his version of your play, but I find it strange that he made no attempt to rearrange Rose's story. Her behaviour in Act Four, Scene One, is enough to make a Marxist weep. She starts by thinking that she is going to marry the Captain, but ends being packed off to round up her sweethearts for recruits with the unlikely promise of a ticket for a play. There's worse to come: Plume appears to renounce his claims to Rose in favour of the new young hearty who so rudely and immediately takes advantage of her. This is confusing and both Rose and Bullock need to know where they stand. 'But will you be so kind to me, sir, as the Captain would?' Rose enquires. Bullock is sensitive enough to realize that haggling on this subject can give great offence to the gentry, but nonetheless shows himself a dogged and determined protector of his family's most priceless asset: 'Dunna be angry sir, that my sister should be mercenary for she's but young.'

In fact, it is probably Bullock who insists upon some form of marriage ceremony between Wilful and Rose. They seem to have had a rather high-spirited and drunken evening with Bullock telling jokes by the bedside ('What jokes' Ron Cook wonders) and Silvia doubtless postponing the moment when her poor performance in bed will be revealed. The next morning (Act Five, Scene One) it all ends in tears. Rose, aware that in the town's eyes she is now a whore, is bitterly disappointed: 'I wonder you could have the conscience to ruin a poor girl for nothing.' But worse is to follow with the bitter irony of arrest on a charge of immorality. What a ghastly twenty-four hours for a poor girl who has hitherto led a blameless life. She begins by selling chickens in the market place and ends up married to Jack Wilful, who she doesn't really fancy and who turns out to be a lousy fuck.

If Brecht were to follow through the imperative of market

124

forces, it would lead to a less kindly and more cynical version of Rose's story. Here the poor girl's ruin would turn into a harlot's progress, which would end with the blowsy Rose running Shrewsbury's first massage parlour. There would be special dispensation and licensing arrangements from Justice Balance; Brother Bullock would be the bouncer; Plume would be a favoured client and possibly an investor, while even Worthy would not be above a discreet visit, when he could slip away from Melinda. But life in a comedy cannot be seen to be so punishing, and I'm very glad, for Rose's sake, that in your version of events, George, Rose ends up safely as Silvia's personal maid – even if this does make for some fairly confusing changes of thought for Mossie. She solved this problem today by selecting Rose's own confusion as a predominant motif. Her last line in the scene is 'We shall find you at home, noble Captain?' and she plays the confusion of somebody trying to find something to depend on in an ever more slippery world. I think the action is 'pins' but it could be 'suspects', depending on the level of awareness we opt for.

Of course, George, I'm well aware that what we're involved in here is a comedy of manners and it is the collision between Plume's sophistication and Rose's ingenuousness that provides much of the humour.

If it doesn't we will certainly have got something wrong. But, at this stage, the way for Mossie to link up the different splodges of her story is to take her moral dilemma very seriously. The more dreadful her situation, the funnier it will appear.

## Sunday 3rd July
### Fourth Weekend

## Dear George,

What about sound? I have to take some decisions about music so I've been forcing Philip Howard to listen to hours of military marches. He has become an expert; and today I listened both to modern military music and to some with eighteenth-century instrumentation. Neither seems right, perhaps because any military music seems too evocative of the establishment. In fact, recorded music at the beginning of the play could be redundant, as you clearly give Kite and the drummer such a great entrance. It could be a mistake to preface this with any other music. If Jim and Jude enter at the prompt side down the emergency fire exit, it will also act as an emergency echo chamber amplifying and magnifying the sound, as well as making it mysteriously hard to locate. It should be a surprising and theatrical kick-off. Jude's drumming has become very good and he's well on top of the Grenadier March, which has a curious offbeat rhythm and, in addition, he's now often on time for rehearsal. What about other sound? I would quite like some birdsong in the scenes by the river or maybe some noises of beasts in the market place? Maybe a carillon of bells summoning people to Evensong, an evocation of England at some point. But when? At the top of the second half? But then why use recorded sound when we've used live sound earlier? How could you have done birdsong? With pipes blown into a bowl of water as in Shakespeare's day? A play of Thomas D'Urfey (of whom more later) specifies that 'Variety of Bird are heard singing' (*Cinthia and Endimion 1696*). Could all the sound we need be made live without the use of any recording? I know Jim does a wonderful young owl and Ron has an entire repertoire of dogs. I must check the company's facility at animal impressions tomorrow. Since we've pillaged the sound budget for the wigs, this could be the way out.

You've been careful to provide musical opportunities within the play. As well as the Grenadier March and the several

126

occasions in Act Two, Scene Three, where Kite and the recruits sing 'Over the Hills And Far Away', there's Plume's own song at the start of Act Three, sung to a tune generally known as The Milkmaids. I know that when you were writing the rivalry between straight drama and musical theatre was at its most intense; the success of the Italian opera was so great that it was thought to be in danger of driving native drama from the English stage altogether. The preface of the Mermaid edition (editor John Ross) records that the opening performances of *The Recruiting Officer* were in repertoire with Bononcini's opera *Camilla* and with Motteaux's semi-opera *The Island Princess*. Here is a letter written by an actor in your Drury Lane Company to a friend back in Nottingham in 1706.

> Our stage is in a very indifferent condition. There has been a fierce combat between The Haymarket and Drury Lane, and the two sisters, Music and Poetry, quarrel like two fishwives at Billingsgate . . . though Farquhar meets with success and has the entire happiness of pleasing the upper gallery, Betterton and Wilks, Ben Jonson and the best of them, must give place to a bawling Italian woman, whose voice to me is less pleasing than merry-andrew's playing on the grid-iron, 'The Mourning Bride', 'Plain Dealer', 'Volpone' or 'Tamerlane', will hardly fetch us a tolerable audience unless we stuff the bills with long entertainments of dances, songs, scaramouched entries, and what not.

The success of *The Beaux' Stratagem* was remarkable not least because it contained no music at all and was thus perceived as a decisive battle in the long campaign between musical and non-musical theatre. So, I've rather anticipated your desires and cut Plume's song in Act Three. I hope that's okay, George. Later editions of *The Recruiting Officer* omit both this song and some of the more farcical passages in the Fortune-Telling scene. Although I'm following in the footsteps of history here, it would not please the upper gallery, who doubtless enjoyed the concessions you made to populism. Our way round this at the Court has been to cut the upper gallery. Part of it is now the lighting box and part of it has become my office. But there's never been too much danger of conceding to populism in Sloane Square.

I wonder what your relationship was like with Thomas D'Urfey? From an earlier generation of dramatists, he had been a principal experimenter with multi-media musical theatre and your preface to *The Recruiting Officer* contains the lengthy and, at first, I thought rather gloating apologia concerning the clash of the first night of *The Recruiting Officer* with the third, or Author's Benefit night of Thomas D'Urfey's *The Kingdom of the Birds* at the rival Queen's Theatre, Haymarket. Apparently, the clash was not to D'Urfey's advantage and his opera closed after a further two performances and with a poorly attended benefit night. It earned under half its production costs. Your preface is stuffed with heavy-handed allusions to the many birds – or actors elaborately costumed as birds – that featured in D'Urfey's epic. Yet, perhaps I'm misreading the preface, or epistle dedication and it contains some regret at so damaging your fellow writer's pocket. I hope so, because D'Urfey has some claim to your goodwill.

Curtis A. Price reckons D'Urfey is 'certainly the most under-rated playwright of the era'. His masterpiece is *The Rise and Fall of Massaniello* (1699). Here is to be found 'the most skilful and ambitious employment of music and ballet of any play of the period'. And it appears, George, that you may be in his debt over a couple of matters: not only is it presumed that you used his re-worked lyrics for Plume's song, 'The Milkmaids', but it is D'Urfey who, in 1706, first printed the tune to 'Over the Hills and Far Away'. This was later used in *The Beggar's Opera* and, together with 'Greensleeves', is one of the few English folk ballads to have truly entered popular culture.

The debate about the importance and significance of music in theatre continues. But the relationship between what is now called 'performance art' and text-based theatre is a hard one. Occasionally they get into bed together, but more often one pushes the other out. Some reckon naturalism to be a dull, tedious thing, synonymous with lack of imagination; while others see the current rush to embrace physicality in our theatre simply as a way of disguising nothing much to say. But it is the struggle to find new form and structure that gives bite to our theatre. I have no first-hand acquaintance with the early years of the Royal Court under George Devine but what is most striking about the body of plays produced then is their whole-hearted willingness to grapple with form, as well as a determination to extend the range of subject matter. There is the mask work in John Arden's *The Happy Haven*, Ann Jellicoe's extra-ordinary linguistic and structural experiments in *The Sport of My Mad Mother* and N.F. Simpson's freewheeling excursions into a particularly English version of Theatre of the Absurd. In these plays actors bark like dogs, turn a bedframe into a piano, transform into aged crones, and a bare space with trestle tables is turned into the teeming kitchen of an hotel. Experiment without content is mindless, but content without structural innovation can be a dull dog indeed.

So, as you crowingly put it, Thomas D'Urfey and his birds were put down by your single Kite. But there are no permanent victories in the theatre and even in a heady moment of triumph it's best for one school of theatre to acknowledge the possibilities of another.

*Dear George,*

I'm glad you weren't in rehearsal today. It could have been one of those days when relations get a bit strained. I don't lose my temper but I do get sharp. I realized today that if this had been a commission I would have been demanding a few re-writes over the last weekend. As I mentioned earlier, in the Court scene (Act Five, Scene Five) you introduce four new characters. Nor does the Court scene have any consistency of stance from the writing point of view. I still can't make it work with any reality at all, and I don't think this is entirely my fault. Frankly, George, this kind of sloppy, non-specific comic writing just isn't on. The scene promises so much more than it delivers. It should provide both a climax of the plot in the confrontation between Silvia and Balance, and a public scene as sharp and pertinent as the Recruiting scene in Act One. I'll bet Bill Gaskill found the scene disappointing too. I'm tempted to ring him but, so far, since rehearsals started, I've resisted calling him. It's hard to tell what you're after. Actually it's not: it's probably that I would like it to be a satirical exposé of corruption with Silvia discovering the unacceptable face of her father's power, and you have nothing more in mind than a genial picture of rustic incompetence. The real weakness is that you don't permit the accused rustics the dignity of their own defence. Your main interest, and indeed ours, is never principally with the lower-class characters. But in previous scenes you do present them with both wit and insight, so that, although we identify with Kite and Plume, we are also able to feel for Costar Pearmain and Tummas Appletree. Here you present the rustics merely as stupid and there is nothing to be done with them.

Balance: Are you married, good woman?

Woman: I'm married in conscience.

Kite: May it please your worship she's with child in conscience.

Scale: Who married you, mistress?

Woman: My husband – we agreed that I should call him husband to avoid passing for a whore and that he should call me wife to shun going for a soldier.

The most noted passage in this scene concerns a miner having 'no visible means of a livelihood, for he works underground'. It seems a bit thin. And, as for Kite's suggestion that the wretched collier's wife should 'go with us to the seaside and there if she has a mind to drown herself we'll take care that nobody shall hinder her' . . . well, is this supposed to be a joke, George? The credibility that you give to the Recruiting scene makes it both cruel and funny: moreover it could only have been written by somebody with first-hand experience of recruiting. The Court scene frankly could have been written by anybody with first-hand experience of somebody else's Court scene. A certain writer's fatigue sets in midway through Act Five. Scenes get shorter, and the originality and purpose give way to a world of theatrical cod that is familiar in any period. I'm frustrated and angry because I can see a wonderful scene within reach but, without your help, I can't make it happen.

Nor could I this afternoon. We return to Roy Porter who emphasizes the JP's 'extraordinarily wide and unsupervised judicial powers'. They could define and punish drunkenness, vagrancy or profanity. So, Balance should be a terrifying and arbitrary figure. We worry away at the scene all afternoon and try to find some reality to cling to. It's not as though there are enough jokes in the scene to give it an alternative shape. What kind of warrant has Balance given to the Constable? Who is outside ready to swear a rape against Silvia/Wilful? How shocked is Silvia by the corruption? How shocked is Balance at Wilful's anarchic behaviour? How hard do Plume and Kite have to work to get their recruits? We've cut Justice Scale but what kind of resistance does Balance get from Justice Scruples' arguments? We impose some sense of proportion on the crimes that are cited. In Shrewsbury's moral canon, poaching outweighs almost everything, even murder, certainly rape, as an horrendous crime. Back to Porter: 'A justice might well be punishing poachers of his own game; after all they were bastioning their own interests with legal sanctions.' So, Kite, who has picked up a considerable body of information during his week's stay, knows exactly the accusation that will incense Balance. We change Balance's 'Send that woman to the House of Correction' to 'Silence or we send that woman to the House of Correction' which, apart from Bickerstaffe in the first scene, is the first major re-write, George. It sounds more likely, less callous and we can't spare Mossie from the scene anyway.

By teatime the scene at last begins to bend. It sounds grittier, and Lesley has hit her stride as the Sidney Carton of Shrewsbury. The scene becomes an emotional climax for her as she is able to release feelings of anger and frustration as Wilful that she would never permit herself as Silvia.

Peter Hartwell has talked of placing a small platform in front of the stage in the place of the front row. This will be where Kite speaks from in the first scene and it can also be used as the dock here. The staging looks epic with Lesley playing most of the scene with her back to the audience. Her wholehearted commitment to the tentative line we've discovered begins to make sense of the scene. The justices sit on the village pump in the centre of the stage. I reassure the actors that this will be okay. Inwardly, I'm unconvinced, but Peter tells me that if they wear magisterial black gowns it should cover the pump altogether.

And, while I'm about it, what about the loose ends, George? Kite has a naff exit with the Constable at the end of this scene never to reappear. At least Brecht solved this problem rather more gracefully. In his final scene, Kite is very chilly with Plume for deserting and returning to civilian life.

By the end of the day, the scene has progressed from A to A and a half – via Z. I admit to the actors that it's not really been my day and I've been directing like a dead turkey. Ron and David and Lesley pick themselves off the floor and go to do their final performance of *Greenland*.

# Tuesday 5th July

*Fifth Week in: Act V Sc. iii*

## Dear George,

I'm back at the Reconciliation scene between Worthy and Melinda this morning, and I enjoyed rehearsing today nearly as much as I found yesterday painful, arid and frustrating. I don't find bad days any better, just easier to own up to. Thank God, I don't have to hide my own incompetence any longer. When I began directing, my whole energy was devoted to concealing the yawning pit of my ignorance. The moment I feared more than any other was admitting that I didn't know: didn't know how to do the scene; didn't know how to direct the play. The fear was of being found out. Now it's sometimes healthy to lay down the reins. It's certainly a relief. The emergency can provoke an anarchic but energized and fruitful discussion, from which something can be harnessed. It's important to learn to control rehearsal: but sometimes it's as important to have the ability to lose control.

The first play I ever directed with professional actors was *Double Double* by James Saunders at the Traverse Theatre in Edinburgh. Set in a bus garage, the central metaphor was a conductor and a driver for ever looking for each other, without much hope of success, as both were played by the same actor. Every night, I used to drive one of the actresses home. Her name was Susan Williamson and she was married to Henry Woolf. She used to tell me where I was going wrong; that Toby should be dominating Scene Two, not George, and that Heather really should be placed more centrally for Scene Four. The advice was very good, and the next day in rehearsal I would shamelessly effect all her suggestions. The actors were surprised and gratified at my competence. That night I would drive Susan home again and hoover from her brain details for the next step. 'Well, now you've got Toby running the scene at last, you really must tell him to find a character . . .', and so on. I think I began to fall in love with actors in that first production, and I've never really been scared of them ever since, which is, I

133

think, a great help to a director. I am still in wonder at their skills. Their talents are always the tools the director uses to crack open the nut of the play.

This morning, we were still having problems in getting Linda to release her anger with Worthy at the moment in the scene when he turns her attempt at a reconciliation into yet another witty and vindictive dispute. The characters were fine, the actions were being played, but the issue was somehow not really releasing Linda's imagination. She kept losing her lines at the climatic moment of the scene; a sure sign with such a talented actress that the moment wasn't being thought through properly. I asked them to play the scene with cockney accents; without spelling it out, I had in mind that both Robert Sideway and Liz Morden, the two characters that Linda and Nick are to play in *Our Country's Good*, are Londoners. The result was shocking; the secret and forbidden spring that links sexuality and violence was released. The scene was energized. It was possible that Linda might launch herself at Nick or that Nick could belt Linda, and that neither of these gestures was very far from a passionate embrace. The physical restraints we had, quite reasonably, adopted had somehow come to inhibit the scene. I turned the actors back into your characters, and Linda's attempt to mollify Nick, following the loss of her temper, led to an immediately repressed touch of his arm, then to a delicate and trembling mutual kiss, followed by a dizzying and heartfelt knee-trembler of an embrace that left both characters gasping for breath and grasping the furniture. It made me laugh, but it was also very moving because it seemed so truthful. These are two inexperienced lovers whose own neurosis and fearfulness has kept them apart. I somehow feel that their marriage could be more stable and constant than that of Plume and Silvia. But that is to look unfairly beyond the bounds of your comedy.

Did two more scenes this afternoon. Beginning to move faster. They look like scenes from the same play. Did the Court scene again. At least it didn't move backwards.

# Wednesday 6th July

## Fifth Week's Rehearsal: Act I Sc. ii

## Dear George,

After my perky day yesterday, I was bold enough to confront one of the other scenes I've been having problems with. So, we worked through the play to the end and then went back to the initial meeting between Melinda and Silvia (Act One, Scene Two), which we've never really got right. I have already cut Silvia's long speech about Melinda's 'airs' and pretensions and this does help to get the scene off to a more fluent start. I asked Linda to describe the setting since we will never see that in the play, and she took us on an imaginary tour of her apartments, which overlook the Market Square. She explained that she was in the process of buying a new house; that Shrewsbury was awful for buying anything decent, and that everything had to be ordered from London. She thought that real fashion would be wasted in Shrewsbury so she's simply decided on co-ordinated upholstery. It sounds very 'Habitat'.

We start well, but soon become bogged down again. It doesn't seem like a difficult scene but I get crosser and crosser as once more it get less and less clear where we are heading. Both Lesley and Linda bring too much energy to the scene and I can't unravel it. I try to locate which character is running, or energizing, each section; we divide the scene into eight units or chunks with quite simple titles like 'Melinda wants to impress Silvia' or 'Silvia wants to focus Melinda'. It goes Melinda/ Silvia/Melinda/Silvia/Silvia/Melinda/Silvia/Melinda. In other words, there is a great competition for dominance, and the responsibility for leading the scene changes hands more often than any other in the play. This is part of the difficulty; it's very easy for the scene to charge away and simply become a very generalized row.

'Constancy' is the hot subject and Silvia is using the word in the sense of fidelity. She is bravely confiding to Melinda that the prospect of Plume's possible future infidelity does not put her off marrying him as she rates other male qualities as far more important. This is a shocking thing to say because chastity would normally be a girl's best friend and virtually her only insurance policy. This threatens Melinda and makes her cross. She thinks Silvia is talking the most outrageous bollocks and is simply rationalizing her passion for Plume. I think Melinda is right and that the scenario goes something like this.

Silvia has spent a frustrating summer at Aston Balance, fretful and irritated with no male or female company of her own age or class. She fantasizes endlessly about Plume, scanning the newspapers for news of his regiment. She perfects her shooting and wins thirteen red rosettes in local gymkhanas. News of the victory at Blenheim reaches Shrewsbury on August 23rd and filters down to Aston Balance on August 24th. Silvia is desperate for news of Plume's survival. On September 15th she hears the amazing story that Kite is in Shrewsbury and that Plume is expected that week! She persuades Balance to pack up and move back to Shrewsbury; this is probably a bit difficult because grouse shooting has just begun. However, they arrive back in town on Tuesday September 20th, with Balance fully alerted to the depths of his daughter's passion. Her first act is to dispatch a footman round to her rival, Molly, with a cheque for 10 guineas (£330). This conspicuous demonstration of noble and generous feelings is calculated to impress Plume with the new philosophy that Silvia has devised over her long, tedious summer at Aston Balance. For she has determined that she will have Plume at whatever cost, and will never let him leave Shrewsbury without her. This is the news she has come to confide in Melinda. Thus the most important line in the scene comes when Melinda observes 'I'm told your captain is come to town', and Silvia responds with steely purpose 'Aye, Melinda, he is come, and I'll take care he shan't go without a companion.' Plume is to encounter as much resolution and determination in Shrewsbury as he ever found on the battlefield of Blenheim.

I am however writing all this to you at 1.30 a.m., and I was quite unable to analyse it in rehearsal. So, what it comes down to is that the row that erupts between Silvia and Melinda is not simply a clash of personalities, it's much more deeply rooted in a conflict over fundamental morality. I see. Now all that remains to be done is to do it.

Linda is worried that her dislike of Plume is becoming too much of a motivating force in her character. Lesley is worried that she can make Wilful masculine, but can't make Silvia feminine enough. I'm just worried about everything.

# Thursday 7th July

### Fifth Week's Rehearsal

## Dear George,

Sometimes I wonder what you made of the English. You didn't come to England till you quit the Smock Alley Theatre in 1697, following the incident when you wounded your fellow actor in a stage duel. How astonishing London must have seemed to you at twenty-eight. Some of that amazement is seen through the eyes of Roebuck, the Irish hero of *Love and a Bottle*. He is shocked at the sight of so many attractive women in the streets of London. 'Oh Venus! all these fine stately creatures!' he exclaims, running out into the street after them. I remember Adrian Dunbar (he'll be playing you in the movie of these letters) telling me how surprised he was that there were so many men with good teeth and so many fine-looking women, when he first came to London from Enniskillen. He felt self-conscious and awkward. Clincher Junior from *The Constant Couple* is a more conventional country bumpkin, and is induced to believe that various ladies of quality are whores, a jolly conceit. Nonetheless, my guess is that you had little difficulty in writing from his point of view. But, although you were in amazement at London, I don't believe you were ever easy here. After the first flush of success, the competitive nature of the metropolis must have been overwhelming, and your failure to earn a real living as a writer demoralising: 'This Poverty, how it makes a Man sneak!' you write with feeling. And you wrote nothing of great significance for the next five years, after your early success with *The Constant Couple* in 1699. It was your recruiting service in Lichfield and Shrewsbury (1705) that released your writing. The two great comedies are set in each of these two country towns and reflect your pleasure at finding another England.

In Shrewsbury, you would have been perceived as a metropolitan sophisticate, and not as a provincial failure from Derry who hadn't really made it. Certainly in the Epistle Dedicatory you make a fulsome acknowledgement of Salopian hospitality:

'The kingdom cannot show better bodies of men . . . more good understanding, nor more politeness, than is to be found at the foot of the Wrekin.' You go further in spelling out your purpose and in reassuring your hosts that they will not be held up to ridicule: 'People were apprehensive that, by the example of some others, I would make the town merry at the expense of the country gentlemen. But they forgot that I was to write a comedy, not a libel; and that whilst I held to nature, no person of any character in your country could suffer by being exposed.' This determination to draw from experience shows the originality of your method. And I think your reassurance is accurate too. Where you are able to 'hold to nature' the picture of the country gentlemen is clear and exact. *The Recruiting Officer* represents a major departure in realism for it is the first major English play that gives a serious picture of country life and not an assemblage of rustic eccentrics designed to titillate the metropolitan palate. In most Restoration drama the country is equated with stifling stupidity. This is why I still quarrel with the Court scene, because here you seem to depart from your declared premise and to present a bullying and corrupt justice in the pursuit of some rather coarse comedy. I wouldn't mind so much if you had provided lines elsewhere in the play that could give life and sense to this particular vision of justice. Nor am I asking for total consistency; on the contrary, a bit of inconsistency gives depth and perspective to a character. But total contradiction, George, leads only to confusion.

Elsewhere, the picture is precise, and reflects the warmth of your feeling about your time in Shrewsbury as well as being a canny Irish assessment of what the English love to hear about themselves. Balance is the very model country gent. He is a liberal, patriotic, paternal, perceptive, tolerant and lively member of the local establishment. He drinks with the young men ('I'm yours over a bottle or what you will') and, although he had an eye for the girls when a young man, settled down to become 'the most constant husband in the world'. Presumably, he must now be one of the most eligible men in Shrewsbury since his wife died when Silvia was four. You don't tell us much about his recent sexual exploits. But my point is that this is how the English have always loved to see themselves, and that by giving them that picture you're on a fair road to charm them to bits.

*Dear George,*

I seem to have been dashing about all week from scene to scene without achieving much. I'm having mid-rehearsal despair rather late in the day this time round. There usually comes a weekend in the middle of rehearsal where I realize that the work has been shallow, inconclusive and wretched, and that my grip on the play is frail and tenuous. A cycle of misery follows: adrenalin pumps, can't sleep, two valium, three hours' sleep, dull day in rehearsal, exhaustion, early night, renewed resolution. Sometimes this cycle is prolonged over a whole week. This hasn't quite happened on your play, but I am beginning to feel knackered. This is a marathon rehearsal period: thirteen straight weeks with rehearsal of one play leading straight into the next, with only a technical rehearsal, previews and an opening in between. Nor is it possible to slow the pace: it's like running a quarter mile and then finding out at the end that you have to run an extra two laps. Rehearsal becomes an endurance test; and stamina becomes a requirement for a director. Real life gets put on hold when you're in rehearsal and the boundaries of existence become simply a journey to the rehearsal room and back. Everything becomes focused on July 26th, or October 12th, or whenever the opening date is. Even the end of term in my first years at boarding school did not provide a date of such significance. I've no idea what's happening in real life, I've lost track of the County Championship, and the clothes I wear every day get drabber and more colourless. I've run out of socks; nor can I eat much. It's as if I want to shrink and become simply a function - a director with no identity or purpose beyond getting the play on. My most desired wish would be to dispense with food, sleep and union regulations, and have the ability and appetite to rehearse continually. Time becomes the most precious commodity and is measured not in hours and minutes but in units of how long it takes to work through a scene. This grim determination can be counter-productive; when I get back to the theatre in the evening my haggard look is often interpreted by the staff as heralding the next Royal Court disaster. 'I didn't think it was so bad after all', offered the YOP Trainee Electrician helpfully at the dress rehearsal of a recent production. I fear the worst because I know the best is impossible. No reaction to this production can possibly co-exist with my expectations. As I peer down the narrow corridor that leads to July 26th, I'm absolutely clear that the impact of my production of your play ought to necessitate an immediate re-write of twentieth-century dramatic history. Anything less will be a major upset. That's why all directors are left flat and hungover following an opening. They're always disappointed. No response from critics, friends or public can match the obsessive importance the event has assumed in their lives. Like you, I've had some terrible and humiliating reviews, but I've also had brilliant ones. Harold Hobson, a generous but eccentric critic, once wrote of a Stanley Eveling play I had directed, 'Mr Eveling, Mr Stafford-Clark, Mr Haygarth and Miss Carpenter make the profession of drama critic the most noble known to man . . . all London should pack this theatre till the walls burst.' I was still disappointed. 'Why didn't he review it seriously,' I carped. The truth is that the process of rehearsal creates an hermetically sealed world for a limited period of time. Sometimes if things aren't going right, this world can be as hideous as a prison camp, but more often, as on this occasion, it provides comfort, shared purpose, comradeship, serious intention, and really good fun. It's like a world in which magic and creation can happen. It's also like a second childhood from which it is traumatic to emerge.

We're rehearsing at the moment in St Gabriel's Parish Hall, which is situated in a time warp somewhere on the Churchill Estate in Pimlico, or Pim-Lee-Co, as we called it when we rehearsed *Fanshen* there sixteen years ago. It has barely changed since, with the same terse custodian to drive us out at 6 p.m. sharp, the same drips from the leaking roof, and the same junk piled round the walls for Saturday afternoon's jumble sale. There was a period of some years when I was off St Gabriel's. I just couldn't rehearse there: too many defeats, too much passion, too much blood on the walls. After an unhappy rehearsal period it becomes obligatory to change rehearsal rooms.

I read one detail which brought me close to your rehearsal conditions. Edward Everard's memoirs describe morning rehearsals at Drury Lane in winter and the necessity to keep moving in order to keep warm. It must have been freezing on that huge stage with no heating, just as it is if we have to rehearse on the Royal Court stage in winter. Overcoats and, often, gloves are obligatory in February and March.

The actors are beginning to winge for a run-through, but I'm not keen on that just yet. We've worked through the whole play twice, and we're now midway through the first half for the third time. A run-through is simply a statement of the current account of accumulated detail. It shows you what you've done so far. If you know you haven't done enough, the time is better spent in accumulating more precision. It's not as though the structure of the play is up for re-examination. I sense that there will be a problem in holding the narrative in the second half, and that the final act is a bit sporadic. But I know that without having to run the play. It's true that some of the company's character work would benefit from a run-through. It would help them to find the arc of their characters: Lesley is still foraging about for Silvia, and Ron hasn't found a character for Brazen yet. I think Brazen is very difficult; the jokes are a bit arcane and the character of fop remains culturally remote for us. I had resisted making him very cowardly, but I think Ron's inclination to take him in that direction is probably right. Maybe we could run Act One on Tuesday or Wednesday next week. From now on the pace of rehearsal accelerates, as we begin at least to run whole scenes. I think we're doing well: the actors are beginning to inhabit the play. The early work on eighteenth-century history is precious as the actors begin to dwell inside the moral attitudes they are expressing.

## Saturday 9th July
### End of Fifth Week

*Dear George,*

During the course of last week all of the cast have been to Her Majesty's Prison, Wormwood Scrubs, to see a performance by the prisoners of Howard Barker's *Love of a Good Man*. I went tonight for the final performance. The prisoner/actors had been supplemented by two professional actresses, and by one professional actor, who had been drafted in to replace a member of the cast who had been transferred to Wakefield high-security nick. It was an instructive occasion. We waited outside the prison gates in a kind of bus shelter while we were issued with passes. After a long wait, the big doors slid apart with a hiss and we went through. The doors closed behind us and we were in a kind of airlock. We were counted again and our passes examined. We were a strange collection. Howard's play had been deemed unsuitable for consumption by fellow prisoners, so the audience was stuffed with theatrical potentates invited by ILEA. Half the audience seemed to be casting directors. There was Mary Selway, hello Patsy Pollock. I learned afterwards that the professional actors were rather over-awed by this unanticipated event. From being a rather peculiar fringe gig, this job had become a major showcase opportunity. I'd never been in a prison before. Fielding once said nobody who had been to an English public school would ever feel out of place in a prison. How right; through the second airlock and it was immediately familiar territory. It was like playing an away match at one of the rather rugged schools, like Sedbergh, where they all wear shorts the whole time. It smelt of disinfectant and bottled male misery. The performance took place in the classroom block next to the kennels, where the prison dogs were kept. So the play was accompanied by howling dogs. Very Howard Barker.

The production was clear and simple, with a minimum of props and lights. I spent part of the time wondering which the prisoners were and what they had done. All of them were Lifers from the Scrubs' D-Wing. The prisoners weren't exactly hard to spot. Two of them were very striking indeed; tall, thin and incredibly pale, they looked like great skinny plants forced to shoot up to find the light. They performed with varying degrees of skill but with intense focus and commitment. Clearly the performance was of great importance to them. Its sexuality was tangible. The play didn't have the frequent references to dripping genitalia that characterise most of Howard's work, but it wasn't lacking in robust sexual expression either: 'I'd like one of her muff hairs to put in my tobacco tin' was one gem, or 'I'd crawl across half a mile of broken glass just to sip her dirty bathwater'. There was no kissing in the play, but there was one tantalizingly close moment. 'I'd like to kiss your white arse,' murmured the gangling, pale intense prisoner as he clasped his hands on the neatly suited buttocks of the extremely attractive actress (Eve White). As his mouth hovered close to hers the charge was tangible. It was difficult to watch. The actors' pride in their work and their pleasure in the achievement was thrilling. Above all, the evening was heady confirmation of how sexy plays are. Keneally spotted that and, of course, he's absolutely right. In an atmosphere of repression and constraint where sex is forbidden, the play becomes a conduit for sexuality. In *The Recruiting Officer* most of the characters are horny most of the time. Given that it remained one of the few expressions of independence for the prisoners too, the rehearsals in Australia must have been crackling with sexual energy.

The actors' exit from the classroom where the performance took place was into a corridor patrolled by two porky screws, who watched the performance with intense disinterest. One of them left his radio on, and the occasional crackle from it mingled with the howling dogs to provide atmosphere background noise. There were three more warders behind me at the back of the room. One of them, the youngest, clapped at the end.

After the performance there was an opportunity to meet the actors for about ten minutes before they were led back to D-Wing. They were eager to talk. There was no shyness or hanging back. Joe, clearly the star of the evening, had killed his best friend when on an LSD trip. I asked him if he wanted to be an actor when he got out. He said he did. I was about to introduce him to Patsy Pollock when I thought to ask when he got out. 'Ten to fifteen years', he said. There didn't seem such a hurry for him to meet Patsy after all. Colin had been a contract killer. The price had been £300. I thought I could afford one

143

or two if that was the going rate. The part of the effete Prince Edward had been played by a chunky, black cockney who had been a body-builder before he came in. He had killed a bloke who had been harassing his sister. Onstage, he seemed charming, witty and rather camp. Offstage, I realized this had been character work of a high order. He was still charming, but definitely not the kind of bloke whose drink you would want to spill in the pub. The men said things like 'Rehearsing is the only time you're not in prison.' They had clearly been obsessed with rehearsing, and wholehearted approval from professionals gave them huge pleasure. They could rehearse for an hour and a half two or three times a week. But rehearsals were often cancelled as screws declined to volunteer for the extra duty, or there simply wasn't sufficient prison staff.

I asked when they were going to do another play. Joe didn't know; he said he could be transferred at any time. He expected to go to Wakefield and there were no drama facilities there. It seemed heartbreaking to awaken this talent and then deny him the possibility of using it. Up close they had a real prison pallor; that's how convicts must have looked when they landed at Sydney Cove after eight months in the hold. They were very emotional. It was, after all, their final performance, and they had been rehearsing since just after Christmas. Joe made a very moving speech thanking the director, Alan McCormack. As they were led away we applauded again; their commitment seemed courageous in this context.

Afterwards we met the professional actors and the director in the prison officers' bar just outside the gates. This was a shock too. It was Saturday night and a country-and-western band was playing. The lead singer was dressed as a scantily clad cowgirl. Somehow the sound of this jollity drifting back to the men, now locked in their cells, was disturbing. The actors were keen to tell us everything: '. . . they approach everything like the SAS. It's their one chance to prove themselves. They never forget a line; and if you lose your lines they prompt you.' Alan McCormack said 'It's the screws that make the prison terrible; they don't think the prisoners should get applause. They're there to be punished. If the prisoners enjoy themselves that's not on.' Exactly the same arguments have been used in our officer's mess scene in *Our Country's Good*. He said the sense of achieving something provided tremendous therapy for the cons: 'It is a total liberation for them.' One problem of directing them was getting them to play anger: '. . . the last time they lost their temper they probably killed somebody.' Eve White told me she and her fellow actress had been treated with extraordinary care and consideration by the prisoners, as if they were china dolls. They had all received first-night presents that the prisoners had made themselves.

An hour or so later I left to go home. As I walked to the car I could hear the prisoners shouting from cell to cell through the warm night. I stopped and listened. Theatre is a savage god, that year by year takes more from you than it ever gives back, but it can be potent and thrilling. And it rewards you when you least expect it.

# Monday 11th July
## Week Six

## Dear George,

Ran the first act today after all. It was good without much danger of careering into brilliance. Ron wasn't happy as Brazen and I couldn't find the notes that would help him. But later in the afternoon he found a voice for Captain Brazen. He started imitating Edward Fox and immediately the status, authority and eccentricity of the character started to flow. Decisions about cowardice or bravery were no longer relevant. For the first time we played a scene and the choices were taken as the character. The decision may not survive the night, but I think it gives us an imaginative base. Lesley was impressive as Wilful, but is still in search of Silvia. She's such a good character actress that she could do anything. Maybe she should go to the General Trading Company and listen to some Sloanes. There's plenty of justification for taking the part in that direction. But this is always the hardest accent to pull off. Most actors can do Cockney or Yorkshire and still retain every moment of emotional truth but it's very difficult to get an edge of Sloane or a county accent without tipping into braying caricature. To attempt Silvia with any kind of middle-class accent could be to invite easy laughter.

The Royal Court is to blame. Plays began with a comic maid dusting flowers and answering the phone with a funny voice. The working class were risible and quaint. Everything was seen from the emotional perspective of the middle-class characters. I once considered reviving an Agatha Christie play simply for discussion about servants and a denunciation of socialism rampant amidst the labouring classes that I had found. It revealed an astonishing amount about class attitudes in the Thirties. Now things have changed so much that it's become rare to see a contemporary play that places a middle-class character at its epicentre. The observation of our writers goes off when they aim at the middle class. Mike Leigh is a wonderful director and his view of working-class and lower middle-class mores is beady

146

and hilarious; but his attempts at middle-class characters seem imprecise and inaccurate. David Hare is one of the few contemporary writers who places middle-class characters, usually women, as the protagonists and instigators of his plays. Certainly I can think of no other modern playwright likely to write a romance set in Shrewsbury inviting us to identify with the emotional life of a wealthy judge's daughter. In your day you had no option. All leading characters had to be middle class. At best, the working class provided robust character roles. Some characters, like Squire Sullen or Tony Lumpkin or Prince Hal, liked slumming it, and then the writer's perspective comes down and slums it with them for a scene or two. Your countryman, O'Casey, is the first playwright I can name with certainty who permits the working class the final dignity of tragedy.

## Dear George,

Just a quick letter this, as I'm working by reflex at this stage of the production, and don't have time to think anymore. I think I'm beginning to smell too as we enter the last lap. I've worn the same Raeboks for six weeks and their sweat tolerance has died. We've also moved to a new rehearsal room in Kennington which makes St Gabriel's Parish Hall seem like a palace. It's like rehearsing in a public lavatory. The acoustics are appalling and it requires a great effort of imagination to summon up Shrewsbury looking at a few old benches and battered packing cases in the middle of a dusty, tiled floor. We seem unerringly to seek out gormet black spots. Not that I long for *haute cuisine* at lunchtime, but I thought Pim-Lee-Co was bad enough. If I don't die of gangrene brought on by poisoned Raeboks I shall do my health permanent damage by a perpetual diet of bacon, egg and chips before we get your play on. Out there in South London menus haven't had to be rewritten in twenty years. Neil O'Malley, the stage manager, eases the pain with periodic infusions of very strong Peruvian coffee, which he brews in a corner of the rehearsal room. He looks after the actors and forces me to take proper breaks. David Haig has taken to rehearsing with his sword on, and as we have no sword belts as yet, he secures it with a complicated Heath Robinson web of twine. Each scene now has a complex sub-plot of which leg he's going to cross when, and where his sword will subsequently fall.

Meanwhile from another rehearsal room upstairs the joyous strains of Declan Donellan's production of *The Tempest* filter down to us. He's been rehearsing here for weeks and while we slum it in the toilet downstairs, he's bagged a pleasant, airy rehearsal room upstairs. The production has lots of music. He's going for the Trevor Nunn upbeat ending, I can tell, and the sound of their merry trampling overhead adds to the dyspeptic churning of my stomach, which has a grim job trying to reconcile too many cups of Peruvian coffee, eggs and bacon, old Raeboks and exhaustion. I'm sure *The Tempest* will be a riotous success, and win every award going. Michael Ratcliffe will fill three columns of the *Observer* with its wonders.

During the day we walk through, and then run, the two long scenes that begin the second half. It all seems rather better than the run through of Act One yesterday. Without the pressure of running it, the actors are able to retain the detail and take charge of their scenes. We make progress. As soon as the quarrel between Plume and Silvia over Rose turns from being an orchestrated piece of business into an undignified and scruffy scuffle it becomes more persuasive. Similarly, when we ran the Fortune-Telling scene yesterday, Jim's peformance as Kite became too much of a performance. He is very funny and was getting the wholehearted approval and encouragement of his fellow actors. But it changes the purpose of the scene. In fact, the real purpose becomes to entertain the audience, and the original intentions of convincing his clients and alarming Melinda and Lucy – all heading toward the superobjective of making as much money as possible – goes out of the window. If you play objectives, it's both real and funny. If you lose sight of this and just aim for funny straight off then you probably miss everything. Still, it's good to have found that out once again.

P.S.   Began to enjoy it again today.

# Wednesday 13th July

## Dear George,

Spent the day working through Act Five. I've always thought it was a particularly hard act, partly because the play begins to wind down, partly because it changes style and partly because of its fragmentary nature. Today none of that seemed to matter, and the progress through the scenes seemed interesting as they were laid out side by side.

I have always thought that you have written a very good play, but today I began to see at first hand that it was a great one. It's like driving a Rolls Royce. It's quite a different sensation to directing a new play. To continue the engineering metaphor, working on a new piece is rather like building a plane that's never flown before; whether or not it will ever take off is a matter of nail-biting speculation. That's not the issue with *The Recruiting Officer* which, as I remember at least three times a week, was the most popular play ever on the eighteenth-century stage. Here the pleasure is of rediscovering a masterpiece. And, at this point, I can begin to feel you taking the weight of the play. It's a wonderful feeling. I remember David Hare describing something similar when he was directing *King Lear* which was his first shot at directing a classic.

The actors are starting to play with authority and take responsibility too. When you work with stars they're inclined to take responsibility too early. They feel they have to, because they know the public are coming to see them. But when you work in the ensemble mode, actors are sometimes inclined to take the weight rather too late in the day. In the early days of Joint Stock I recall Bill Gaskill fretting at what he considered the actors' over-dependence on the director's vision. Not this bunch though.

Today's particular triumph was the Duelling scene (Act Five, Scene Six). Now that Ron is beginning to find Brazen it came swiftly. We found the scene through taking the weapons seriously, and through assessing that Worthy was not really a weapons

150

man. Strictly 3rd XI material. As Nick, playing Worthy, rushes on breathless with a case of duelling pistols, speeding out of his mind on adrenalin and fear. The terrified Brazen does all he can to persuade Worthy to use swords, where at least his superior skills and experience will give him some advantage. But Worthy will have none of it and is pacing off to begin the duel when Brazen tries his final desperate bluff: 'Come, where's your cloak?' Worthy is momentarily confused by this Pythonesque *non-sequitur*, whereupon Lucy reveals her true identity. Following the incident both men are in shock: Brazen releases his by shouting at Lucy. This is the only really angry moment in the play. Meanwhile, Worthy, in post-traumatic shock with wig askew, is dry-retching over a chair. At the end of the scene both men bustle off to resume their lives leaving poor Lucy, whose ambitious plans for self-improvement are totally banjaxed.

I realize again today how much of your play is in the form of asides. The actors have spent a lot of time in rehearsal talking directly to me or the stage management. They have to assume an immediate ease with the audience for this to work and also have to strike a specific relationship. You have given all the principal characters the opportunity to take the audience into their confidence. This gives the play a particularly open quality, for it doesn't progress far without some character enlisting the audience's sympathies directly. Each character treats the public as if they were their own particular friend, sharing the same concerns and moral values. Each is, of course, innocent of the knowledge that every other character also believes they have a special relationship too. 'Tis the greatest misfortune for a woman to want a confidante', moans Melinda, but the same need besets all the characters. Often you place the asides at a moment of particular stress, when the character has real need of an ally. Thus the action is often to 'enlist'. For example, Balance confides his anger that Plume should have, as he thinks, conspired in Silvia's deception (Act Five, Scene Seven). His action is 'to outrage' the audience. Earlier in the play, Silvia engages our sympathy in her agonizing choice between love and money (Act Two, Scene Two). Action: 'to enlist' us. And, at the moment when the drunken Plume is quarrelling with Brazen, Melinda lets us into the deepest secret of all. Action: 'to entrust'. She confides: 'I see Worthy yonder, I could be content to be friends with him would he come this way.' Exercise for tomorrow: who are their best friends? Who does each character imagine the audience are when they enlist their support or entrust their worries? Kite thinks they're fellow cronies in the Sergeants' Mess. Silvia imagines they're chums from the same dorm at boarding school and so on.

# Thursday 14th July
## Week Six: Act V Sc. vii

*Dear George,*

Finished the last scene before returning to the beginning of the second act again. I'll run through the second act tomorrow and then have a first complete run-through on Saturday. We start the technical in the theatre on Monday, final dress rehearsal next Wednesday and first preview on Thursday.

Today, I learned to love the last scene. Of course, the play is a romantic comedy that ends with two marriages. I think I told you that we don't have plays like that any more. In fact, this is the first play I've directed that has romance as the mainspring of its plot. And it's very moving. It's a conclusion that you were quite sharp about on other occasions. In *Love and a Bottle*, when Lovewell asks Lyrick, the impoverished poet, 'What relish have you of comedy?' he replies, 'My curiosity is fore-stalled by a fore-knowledge of what shall happen . . . and as the Catastrophe of all Tragedies is Death, so the end of Comedies is Marriage.' 'And some think that the most Tragical conclusion of the two,' responds Lovewell with fashionable cynicism. In the first scene, Plume ranges himself against marriage and of course, in *The Beaux' Strategem*, you assemble a formidable argument in favour of divorce. But, nonetheless, Balance giving Silvia away to Plume against his own declared self-interest is touching. And their doe-eyed fascination for each other is moving too. Plume's journey in the play is from boyish misogyny to acceptance of the authority of romance. It would be nice to think that Silvia and Plume enjoyed at least a couple of years of bliss before his drinking became a serious problem. 'Constancy', the quality which Silvia affects to despise, but which leads her to her extravagant course of action, is not much valued in our own century either. Of course, you try to have the best of both worlds, by having Melinda undercut the romantic comedy you have just written: 'Your history is a little romantic, cousin,' she says with just an echo of her acerbic bite.

Your predecessors, the Jacobeans, were more concerned with

153

lust than romance, which is why their plays were deemed crude and unsuitable by eighteenth-century theatre managers, who, I'm sure, were assessing their market correctly. Meanwhile, here at the latter end of the twentieth century, we currently have a grim pleasure in doom. Most plays now end pessimistically. The hero does not get the loot or the girl. This is the Eighties. In the Seventies I think we felt it our responsibility to provide a moral uplift and an optimistic ending. Plays were an education. *Fanshen* would be a good example.

It's possible to see this progress through the work of Caryl Churchill. *Light Shining in Buckinghamshire* (1976) certainly ends with elegaic melancholy, but the focus of the play is on the opportunities provided for change by the social unheaval that followed the English Civil War. *Cloud Nine* (1979) is an optimistic look at the possibilities of change and fusion that might be brought about by liberation from sexual stereotyping. Caryl is a socialist and both plays were written when a socialist government was in office. So, in some senses, *Light Shining in Buckinghamshire* can be seen – with the wisdom of hindsight – to be a lament for the opportunities missed. *Top Girls* (1982) was written in the early years of Mrs Thatcher's first term, and ends with Angie's chilling vision of the future for the have-nots in Thatcher's Britain; 'frightening'. *Serious Money* (1987) is a satirical and neo-Jacobean look at a world whose values have been shaped by the imperatives of that government. And her new play, *Icecream* (1989), looks at the pragmatic response to a murder by a group of people whose moral grip is tenuous. Caryl's recent plays are a voice of opposition; opposition not only to the government, but also to the moral climate in which we're living. As the Left has failed to unite and present a coherent critical voice, responsibility for this role has been taken up by theatre and television. *Blind Justice* and *A Very British Coup* as much as *Serious Money* or *Pravda* are the voice of an opposition in exile.

Your situation was very different, George, and although your plays are critical of aspects of the society you lived in, they are, on the whole, plays of celebration. They celebrate an England in harmony with itself. You, Vanbrugh and Mrs Centlivre were the three most successful writers of the early eighteenth century, and you were all Whigs supporting a Whig government who had just won a famous Whig victory. To place a serving officer as hero of a play would have been inconceivable to a Tory writer like Dryden or Swift. In 1710 a Tory ministry came to power again. It was three years after your death. I'm sorry we never got to see your plays of opposition.

P.S.   It's 2.30 a.m. What am I doing writing this? I should be preparing for tomorrow.

*Dear George,*

We're back in our toilet in Kennington tomorrow for our run-through, but today, Bo Barton, the Production Manager, allowed us to rehearse on the stage. This will save an enormous amount of time on Monday when we start the technical. One hundred years old this year, the Royal Court is an extraordinary precise instrument. Seating almost four hundred people on three levels, the compactness of its dimensions give it a humanity which I cherish. It's large enough to be a public stage that can contain the passion of epic work, yet small enough to preserve an intimate relationship between the stage and the auditorium. This is why actors love playing on it, despite the poor sightlines, lack of wing space and terrible salaries. It provides a rigorous test for new work, and it demands standards that in the long run have probably ensured the survival of the English Stage Company, who have been resident in the theatre since 1956.

Peter Hartwell's set is elegant and minimal. There's a slight rake and the decision to turn the two downstage assemblies back into boxes looks inspired. Immediately above them are two smaller boxes positioned right over the stage. As we rehearse the actors take turns to sit there. The view is terrific and the fun of such proximity will make for an occasion. I understood immediately why, in your day, the seats on the stage were the most expensive; it bestows privilege to be up there, an intimate of the artistes. In the centre of the stage is a bench and behind it the village pump. When David washes at the beginning of the play, it will spurt real water. For the scenes in Melinda's apartment or Balance's house, a Georgian window flies between the bench and the pump thus creating an interior. Immediately upstage of the two boxes are two green Georgian doors. By them are placed two straight-back chairs. The doors and the chairs are the only furniture and with them we must create Shrewsbury. It looks very like the Restoration theatre

156

sketched on the pink cover of the New Mermaid edition which we have been using. It's very simple, almost as simple as the carpet Peter Brook used for his storytelling theatre. Upstage, against the back wall, is a perspective of Shrewsbury. It's based on two paintings discovered and bought for the town by Vivien Bellamy, the Curator of Shrewsbury Museum Service. She showed them to us on our trip to Shrewsbury. The painted cloth is behind a gauze and will be revealed as Melinda and Lucy stroll on in Act Three, Scene Two. This is the first time the action moves from the town to the Riverside walks and will, I hope, provide a *coup de théâtre* of a modest nature. The whole set recreates the elegant proportion and style of Georgian theatre and suggests a small country town with wit and economy.

I predict the set will be dismissed or at best remain unnoticed. Peter's work is both unobtrusive and unfashionable. He rarely gets the recognition that I feel he deserves but I love his restraint craft and taste. Peter is Canadian and came over to train at Percy Harris's school. His first job was as an assistant to Jocelyn Herbert, whose designs were so seminal at the Court in its early days; so, in some sense, I feel he continues the tradition of the English Stage Company. I did once attempt to chivvy him into something more fulsome. He explained that if you had been brought up in rural Ontario, where for most of the year the most sumptuous visual image was a single strand of barbed wire across a field of snow it was hard to embrace a fruitier style with any ease.

We worked through the Recruiting scene and the beginning of the second half. The play took to the stage like a duck to water. Most of my notes were to discourage the actors from enjoying themselves so much. In the excitement of being onstage, they began to pitch things too high, so that Silvia's assault on Rose (Act Four, Scene One) became a funny piece of business rather than the arrogant behaviour we had discovered in earlier rehearsals. Similarly, Jim began to display Kite's misogyny at Melinda's expense in the Fortune-Telling scene (Act Four, Scene Two) rather than using it to alarm her. Generally the actors began to let fly with their characters which is probably very good. Lesley's boiling rage in the Courtroom scene (Act Five, Scene Five) set it at a high emotional level. It looked wonderfully anarchic: partly also because Mark's generosity and enjoyment of his fellow actors prevents him from focusing on his own performance and taking charge as Balance should do.

157

As the play begins to take shape and decisions get nailed down, I miss your approval. I like the writer to be in rehearsal all the time, so that they're always part of the process, but their presence is essential at the beginning of the rehearsal when decisions about which route to choose are taken, and, at this point, when a few destinations begin to come into sight.

# Saturday 16th July
## First Run-through

## Dear George,

First run-through today. It was good. A good account of the work so far, but not a spectacular breakthrough. I think the actors were pleased and encouraged. I felt disappointed – not with them, but with myself. Sometimes, after a run-through, the director can *see* the play. Not only see the work that's been done, but see the way ahead and what work remains. What decisions need to be changed. The play reveals itself. It's like climbing a hill in order to view the route. If you attempt a run-through too early in rehearsal, the hill is too low and you won't be able to see much; but if you leave it too late you're dangerously dependent on it being a clear day. Today, it was murky and I couldn't see much. I remember the first run-through of *Rat in the Skull* by Ron Hutchinson and getting from it an instinctive feel of how much more passionate we could make the play. I could see when Brian Cox, who played the central role of an RUC officer, had to drive the piece and when he could afford to relax. It's harder with *The Recruiting Officer* because there is no central figure who drives the action; this responsibility is shared. Now we've begun to run the play it's important the actors understand when it's their turn to run with the baton. The characters who drive the first three acts up to the interval take over from each other like this:

Act One: Kite, Plume, Plume, Silvia/Melinda.
Act Two: Balance, Plume/Silvia, Balance, Worthy, Kite, Plume.
Act Three: Plume, Plume, Kite, Kite, Balance, Worthy, Brazen, Rose, Melinda, Brazen, Worthy, Plume/Brazen, Kite, Brazen.

These are the roles which have the responsibility of energizing the successive scenes. So Act One begins with Kite's recruiting

159

speech. Then there are two scenes run by Plume; first with Kite, then with Worthy, and the act ends with the Melinda/ Silvia scene where the driving force is equally shared. So, it requires a high standard of teamwork and, although Plume is a leading role, it's not like *Hamlet* or even *Rat in the Skull*, where the arc of the evening can be governed by decisions taken by one actor. The ensemble work is coming, although it wasn't entirely there this afternoon. Nor have I put in enough rest points. The action is too continuously frenetic. For example, at the start of Act Three, Plume can relax. The purpose and energy of the previous night's recruiting drive have gone, and it's a moment where we could show 'the fatigue' if not the 'endless pain' of recruiting. It's the next morning. It's sunny. He's hungover. Worthy comes on with the drinks, and they moan about their girlfriends. Similarly, Melinda's entrance (Act Three, Scene Two) should be discontented and bored, but not too fretful and neurotic. We should see her with nothing to do and nobody to talk to except Lucy. And, at the end of Act Three, just before the interval, I can spot a place where we can see Brazen at rest. After the duel, he's busy befriending Plume. In fact, we always see Brazen with his busy public persona and it would really help Ron if we could see him in just a moment of repose. Brazen is too old for all this fighting and sexual rivalry. He should appear tired and vulnerable. When Plume leaves there's no longer any necessity to keep up a front.

After the run, the actors were expectant, with the exception of Ron, who I could see felt disappointed. I knew the notes I had to give hadn't quite caught the run-through and that they would neither help Ron take the next step forward with Brazen, nor quite meet the expectations of the rest of the company. But the run-through had been good under near impossible conditions and I opted for optimism. Here are the notes I took in run-through short-hand. Some of them are very trivial, but I've included them just as they are. The bits in brackets are explanatory additions:

2.08 pm Alford House, Kennington. First run-through.

I i        Jude: Drum roll as noisy as poss

Mossie & Mark & Nick: Not so certain.
Ron v.g. as Salopian bystander

(The style of acting required in the

160

Bickerstaffe prologue should contrast
with the more formal presentation of the
subsequent Plume/Kite scene. Actors
should go for the tentative quality of
overlapping dialogue and docu-realism.
Ron alone hit this style).

Jim & Jude: Teamwork, eyes (They operate
with the practised precision of a busker
and his mate).

Jim: talk (contrast Kite's public speech with
his informal chat to the small crowd)

Jim & Jude: on 'behold a great man' big
drum roll (to re-focus attention on Ron
who is trying on the sergeant's cap)

David: embrace Worthy (should be
physically freer, Plume isn't reticent
about male bonding)

David: news that W proposes to marry Mel
is a shock (Plume can't stand Melinda)

David: 'Sarnt Kite wait on the lady' (is an
order. 'Sergeant' is French for servant
and the relationship between Kite and
Plume is very like master and servant at
times. Neither man is coy about this.)

David and Nick: Scene good. Sounded like
boys' talk.

I ii    Lesley: Don't characterize Silv so yng.
Don't play spoiled brat. Don't push
character away from you. (The answer to
all those questions about having a Sloane
accent is 'no'. Forget about it. It's a juve
lead part not a character role and Lesley
needs to pull the character close to her
and show her own vulnerability.)

Lesley: 'Oh madam!' react straight away.
(to Melinda's insult i.e. don't pause to
absorb it)

161

'Phonsia: earwig (listen to Silvia and
Melinda's conversation more openly)

II i    Mark: play 'shocks' (on 'would not you
debauch my daughter if you could'.
Balance intends to be provocative and
challenging. In a sense he attacks
Plume).

David & Lesley: stiller (the scene should be
taut and still. The shock of meeting
should contrast with the informality and
ease of the previous scene)

II ii   Mark: exc but relish the words 'maggoty',
'devils' (Balance doesn't enjoy upsetting
Silvia and he comforts and teases her as
soon as the scene permits)

Mark: precision with energy (the problem
for Mark lies in characterizing an older
man who still remains an authority figure
and runs most of the scenes he's in. He
must hit Balance's energy without
becoming too 'old party'-ish and
overcharacterizing his age.)

Lesley: gv yrself less time for aside to
audience

Mark: angry but not apoplectic (action is
certainly 'to appal' and 'to shock' the
audience with Plume's behaviour but in
order to 'enlist' their support)

Mark & Nick: Sc. a bit rusty (somehow we
seem to have missed it in rehearsal).

II iii  Jim: 'A queen!' (Kite aware of Pearmain's
unwitting *double-entendre*)

Jim: 'wonderful works of nature' . . .
quieter (Kite should move thro' scene
from boisterous raucousness to maudlin
reverence)

RECUITING
SCENE

Jim: 'nay then I *command* you to stay'.
(emphasis: it's an order)

David: 'Give me thy hand' (more open and
manly. Invite him into the wonderful
enclosed world of the army)

Jude & Linda: be specific (about the sums
of money you've been given)

III i

David: be more boring (this is the rest
point we could take)

Mossie: Rose v.g.

Jim: Kite sp exc (Kite's speech to Worthy
was excellent. Hit quality of brutalized
self-loathing)

Mark: 'Sergeant go along with this fellow
to your captain' (Balance is also an ex-
officer and accustomed to taking
command. He would order Kite)

David and Mossie: CP fine (The Comic
Potential of Plume attempting to
discipline Rose with his sword scabbard,
which extends way behind him while
talking to Balance is not too gross a
piece of comic business)

III ii

Linda & 'Phonsia: sc gd. detail retained.

Jim: Kite chilling (when he warns Silvia of
the dangerous liaisons likely in army life)

David: examining sword (David has added
the excellent detail of checking his sword
after the fight to make sure it hasn't got
chipped)

Ron: end of first half rather unworked.
Moment of repose for Ron here?

INTERVAL

IV i

Ron: v.g. (as Bullock who shows real
concern for Rose's moral appearance)

Ron, Mossie, Lesley, David: Staging (my staging falls to pieces when more than three people are on stage together. It comes from years of minimal casts in impoverished theatres. But this is particularly ineptly staged).

David & Lesley: George's sex jokes v.g. (I bet the bit where Plume kisses Silvia, thinking she's Wilful 'S Death there's something in this fellow that charms me' has always got a huge laugh. It seems irresistibly funny)

David: looks like you know you're kissing a girl (i.e. that's wrong)

Linda & 'Phonsia: not too private (halfway through the scene they sit on the bench and the energy level drops too low)

Linda & Ron: timing v.g. (of whole misunderstanding. Melinda hitting Brazen and imagining he's Worthy. On a couple of occasions the stage directions describe a piece of original staging or comic business. I think we've refound this one)

David: 'Whim' attitude v.g. (Plume dismisses Worthy's unmanly paranoia about Melinda)

IV ii        Jim: Kite's different impersonations are terrif

FORTUNE      Linda & 'Phonsia: sucked in (despite
TELLING SCENE themselves, by the detail of Kite's predictions)

Jim: asides v.g. (George has given Kite the opportunity to keep in contact with the audience all through the scene. This is precious because we see the scene from Kite's perspective. The audience become his friends, Jim uses these asides with great variety)

|            | David: racing (end of scene gets well complicated with detail of who signed what letter. It can't be rushed) |
| V i        | Mossie: Rose's grief shd grow (through this scene and the following scene as she realizes the enormity of crossing the morality gap and the consequences of being caught in bed with Wilful) |
| V ii COURT ROOM SCENE | Jude: Scruple v.g. (Jude characterizes a Salopian pillar of the establishment with élan) |
|            | Lesley: asides v.g. (again we see this scene from Silvia's point of view) |
| V iii      | Linda & Nick: overlap (this is a note for me to effect on Monday and is about the possibility of overlapping scenes. It might work)* |
|            | Linda: not playing from total conviction (that Worthy is going into 'certain danger' and death were he to venture abroad) |
|            | Nick: over-energizing. Let her run the scene. |
| V iv       | David and Jim: naff (my fault. Again this is an under-rehearsed scene whose value we haven't quite located) |
|            | Ron: whisper after 'Married' (Brazen should be aware he's communicating an important secret) |
|            | David: Mel hs *secured* a person already (emphasis. Plume has 'to galvanise' Worthy) |
|            | Nick: You'll get a round (if he can make this instant transformation from Worthy to the Constable) |

*We tried it. It doesn't.

165

Mark & Jude: play real time (the judge's business with papers needs to be thought through and given some reality)

Moss: 'lookee Mr Captain' (this interruption from audience should be fired with more rage)

Lesley: don't slow down too much in Court scene. (The characterization of Wilful is excellent but the energy needed to disrupt established court procedure is considerable.)

David: Articles of War. as fast as poss (the word which needs to reverberate is 'death')

Lesley: 'This is the truth and I'm Ready to Swear it.' Action is 'to convince', you're playing 'scorns'.

V vi

Phonsia: Unmask as you say it ('Come gentlemen I'll end this strife') not after the line

DUELLING
SCENE

Nick: Once Brz has left don't hurry (scene should change pace)

V vii

Mark: Change pace (again, we should return to urgency after the elegaic melancholy that ends the previous scene)

Mark:'I have consented indeed' (needs more time both to re-establish relationship with audience and to absorb the intricacy of his own position)

Mark: spch giving Silvia away v.g. (although the staging went awry somewhat)

David: last spch (has to be lifted, so the play ends on a positive upbeat)

All: ends of both acts are generalized and lacking in focus. We need time to rehearse them.

The actors took the notes well and Lesley absorbed the change of direction for Silvia with enthusiasm. Learning what you can from a director's notes is not the least part of an actor's job. I recall one notes session for *A Mad World My Masters* by Barrie Keeffe, which Bill Gaskill and I directed together. Simon Callow, who hadn't enjoyed rehearsals much and who has since adjusted history by writing his own account of his time with Joint Stock, resisted every note he was given. Bill finally said, in exasperation, 'Simon, you must learn to take a note or you deny the possibility of learning.' This at last silenced the mighty Callow, and certainly impressed me. I admit that I have borrowed Bill's phrase on a couple of occasions.

We split up. The company were cheery and have something to think about over the weekend. I know Ron will keep worrying away at it. Next time we meet it will be onstage in costume. I drove back to the Court to find we had no lighting designer. Andy Phillips has walked out.

*Dear George,*

Slept all morning. Bo phoned to say that Chris Toulmin, the Royal Court's chief electrician, will replace Andy Phillips as lighting designer. Andy has walked out on several shows during previews before, but has never failed to make the starting line. This is a first even for him, but his capacity for self-destruction is equalled only by his talent. He's a wonderful lighting designer, capable of sculpting figures in light out of the darkness, or of uncovering the pulse and rhythm of a show by the way he orchestrates the movement of light from one scene to the next. Twenty years ago he was chief electrician at the Royal Court, where he learned and developed his skills. He has a fierce, emotional loyalty to the Royal Court's past and a fairly ambivalent attitude to its present. His heart lies with the great directors of the Royal Court's youth – Lindsay Anderson, Bill Gaskill and above all John Dexter – and he regards me as, at best, some interloper with squatter's rights in Sloane Square, unable to match the mighty deeds of the past. (Certainly my relationship with Lindsay has always been strained. At the time when I started to direct at the Court he was a dominant and influential figure who was unable to conceal his hostility to the work of a younger generation of writers. 'Do you really think this is a good play?' he barked across the bar in the interval of the first preview of Howard Brenton's *Magnificence*.) The mythology of the past is an oppressive weight for the director of the English Stage Company as I'm sure it is for the director of the Moscow Arts Theatre or the Abbey Theatre, Dublin. The temptation to use the glorious achievements of the past as a club to belabour the puny efforts of the present is irresistible to any critic in a sour moment. But, on the other hand, it sets extraordinary standards.

Andy lit the first production I ever directed at the Royal Court, *Slag* by David Hare. Over the final act there was a slow sunset reflected in the window of John Gunter's set. I thought it was very beautiful, but Bill Gaskill, the then Artistic Director, thought it sentimental and irrelevant and told me so after the first preview. The next morning I tentatively broached the subject with Andy. He looked pensive, sipped his first vodka of the day, and gave me some brilliant tactical advice: 'If you cut it now, he'll only be on to you about something else tonight. Why not leave it and cut it after the last preview?' This plan worked well: every night Bill would bully me about the sunset to the total exclusion of any other matter. After the final preview we cut it. Bill was delighted and congratulated me on the wisdom of the decision.

After yesterday's run-through, the play began to take shape in my mind and I have a fairly clear idea of what needs to be done.

It's a great play, George.

It's also a bit reppy: that is, you can see how the play is built for a leading man (Plume), a soubrette (Melinda) a 'heavy' character actor (Kite), a comic (Bullock), a younger character actress (Rose) and so on. This is why I now see that Lesley can't make Silvia 'a character' in the same way say that Mossie can with Rose. Those archaic divisions in the casting director's bible, *Spotlight* – Leading and Younger Leading Women; Character Women; Younger Character Women; and Young Actresses – have always seemed arbitrary and rather quaint; certainly irrelevant to most of the casting that I do. I now see that they provide an accurate working analysis and casting breakdown for classical work.

# Monday 18th July
## Technical Day One

## Dear George,

First day of the technical. It should take two days to work through the play onstage, working on the lighting as we go, examining the costumes, which have previously only been seen in fittings, and looking at the props, furniture, sound effects, entrances, exits, sightlines, blocking, costume changes and wigs. All this won't leave much time for acting, but it should be possible to re-orchestrate some of the moments that we spotted on Saturday. Because Chris Toulmin needs the morning to set lights, we start the technical three hours late. Peter Hartwell and I swear never to work with Andy Phillips again.

The privacy of the rehearsal room has gone for ever. In the afternoon, we start new working relationships with three electricians, two dressers, a wig dresser, a production manager, a wardrobe mistress, an assistant wardrobe mistress, a master carpenter, a deputy master carpenter, and that phenomenon of the Eighties, a YOP trainee assistant. Their involvement and commitment is essential over the next three days. As I've mentioned before, many plays that have been exciting and original in rehearsal leave these qualities in the rehearsal room. The reverse can happen too: a production on which the intermittent word leaking from rehearsal has been misery and despair can be pulled into some sort of shape by a director able to use the technical. A director needs to focus on quite different priorities and develop a different range of skills during these three days. Above all, the director has to be pragmatic and objective. He has to reassess the staging and be ready to discard even the most treasured moments if they don't work.

We have some early successes: Linda is very pleased with Melinda's wardrobe and Lesley Sharp looks very good in a russet-coloured riding habit and her wig is a triumph. Usually, I'm wig-resistant. It gives me more pleasure to have even the most difficult transformations accomplished by the actors' skills rather than have them depend on any theatrical device. But Peter and Lesley have persuaded me that a hairpiece will help Lesley as Silvia and make her wigless appearance as Wilful even more startling. She's cut her hair off. We don't get as far as Wilful's entrance today, but certainly the wig (£400 worth) gives her great confidence and leads her to Silvia's classy arrogance without straining. Ron looks great too. He has a fluffy white wig dressed out at the sides. And raised heels. He worries that it makes too strong a statement. We'll see. But I think it looks fine.

During the course of the day, I go a bit wild with the offstage animal noises. Having decided to use no recorded sound at all I determine that any sound effect should be created live. So, the clocktower of St Chads is Neil O'Malley on tubular bells. Lesley Sharp's first contribution to the evening is a solo upon the woodcock pipes that presages Plume's arrival in Shrewsbury, and Ron Cook orchestrates a battalion of dogs who bark in response to the rowdy Recruiting scene. But the one that really makes me laugh is at the start of Act Three. This follows the Recruiting scene and marks the moment where Plume is having an early-morning drink with Worthy. It's one of the places where I was looking for a rest point after Saturday's run-through. Plume now enters slowly by himself and sits down at the pump to the sound of lowing cattle. He looks around in distaste as Jim's ewe calls plaintively for her bleating lamb. The forlorn lambkin is played by Nick, who then immediately enters with the round of drinks. He says it's the first time he's bleated *before* he goes onstage . . . but it seems very good psychological preparation for his instantaneous costume change from Worthy to the Constable that we will attempt tomorrow.

A solid purposeful first day's technical.

## Dear George,

Two days before the first performance and the advance at the box office stands at £3,237, which is pretty puny. It's certainly not enough to be any guarantee of success or to provide much prior evidence of public interest. Sam Shepard's *A Lie of the Mind* opened to £12,197 and *The Normal Heart*, which did, however, feature Martin Sheen, to £24,549. 'You should have got one or two stars, Max,' David Haig said ironically. The pressure on all of us to make *The Recruiting Officer* a major box-office hit is greater than I can ever remember. Attendance so far this year has been disappointing. I estimate we must be £50,000 down at the box office. But the set and costume budget for *Our Country's Good* has already been consumed by *The Recruiting Officer*, and we're heading for a total overspend on both shows of about £20,000. This means a possible deficit at the end of the year of £70,000. The net cost of presenting four plays in the Theatre Upstairs is £85,000, so a deficit of this size could have an appalling effect on next year's upstairs programme.* In the course of the day, I find a moment to talk to Graham Cowley, the Royal Court's General Manger, and we agree to freeze this year's final production in the Theatre Upstairs until the position is clear. This could give us a possible saving of £22,000. The staff are fully involved in the financial situation and the cast too are well aware of the position. It's impossible to work somewhere as close-knit as the Court and not become involved in its dilemmas.

Three years ago, we were approaching the point where it would be hard to present a full year's work of four plays in the Main Theatre and four plays in the Theatre Upstairs. On this occasion Joseph Papp responded to our plight with a $50,000 Challenge Fund: a dollar for every pound we raised. That year (1985–6), with his contribution, we raised £113,000 towards

---

*It did. The Theatre Upstairs closed on March 25th 1989.

our annual revenue. In the two years since then, *The Normal Heart* and *Serious Money* both played to capacity business and both transferred to the West End. This year, unless either *The Recruiting Officer* or *Our Country's Good* becomes a comparable hit the vulnerability of our real position will stand revealed. For five years the Royal Court has been caught in an argument between the Arts Council, who seek plural funding for their clients and the Royal Borough of Kensington and Chelsea, who see the Royal Court as a national resource, which should be funded nationally. During this time, we've dropped from seventh to sixteenth in the national table of funding from all sources. We now receive public funding on a level with Derby Playhouse and the York Theatre Royal – less than Greenwich, less than Coventry and less than the Lyric, Hammersmith. It's simply not possible to run a national resource for new writing with this level of support.

Doubtless it will seem strange to you that the state should be expected to contribute to the maintenance of the theatre. In your time, the Tory squirearchy needed the spectre of invasion to persuade them to pay even the taxes that raised Marlborough's army, let alone subsidize a theatre. But the truth is that subsidy has created a golden age of writing for the stage in the last thirty years. Playwrights have been able to earn a living. Not many have died impoverished of tuberculosis before the age of thirty in filthy garrets. The theatre has been a medium for serious social debate for the last three decades. Historically, this hasn't often been the case. In the early nineteenth century Byron, Shelley and Coleridge used poetry as a forum for philosophical, political and moral debate, while later in the same century the novel became the great medium for social examination. Theatre doesn't *have* to survive as a serious contributor to culture, although it will probably always survive as entertainment. As I've already noted, your own century shows that market forces are not user-friendly to writers. When theatres expanded, writers were pushed out. As public subsidy has dropped, the Royal Court has become increasingly dependent on raising money. In the last five years we've raised a higher proportion of our turnover than any other theatre in the country except the National Theatre. We've also broken box-office records. In fact, so committed have we become to incentive-funding, marketing and fund-raising, that it's nearly become a heresy to state what is obvious common sense: that without equally committed support from the public sector the Royal Court will not survive. In the end, George, our theatre will be known to posterity by the plays it creates: everything else dies with us. On these grounds alone, the Royal Court is the *most* important theatre in the country; not the seventeenth!

So, under these circumstances, it's understandable that over the last two days the staff have been sneaking in to have a little look at the technical. It is, after all, their jobs that are at stake. So far, most seem cautiously approving. This is good, as the original decision to devote a quarter of the year's production resources to a revival of your play didn't meet with unanimous approval. But it's possible to endure almost any situation at the Court as long as everybody thinks the work is good. When the building's internal verdict is split about the worth of a particular play morale sags alarmingly. There can also be a considerable split between peer-group approval, as exemplified by the building, and public response. *The Normal Heart* was acclaimed by the public but split opinion internally. But, in this particular case, Dr Success overruled any difference. On the other hand, Richard Wilson's production of Robert Holman's *Other Worlds* played to the poorest houses ever known in my tenure at the Court. One night there were seventeen paying customers. But it remains a play particularly valued by everybody who worked here. In fact, the four new boxes that have been created for this production are to be named after glorious productions from the Royal Court's past, and Chris Harding-Roberts, our long-serving master carpenter, asked particularly that one should be named *Other Worlds*.

We finish the technical and manage to get in a run of the first half. Everybody is tired and it looks businesslike rather than inspired; but the costumes look good and the costume changes go well. After six weeks of anxiety, Ron manages the change from Bullock to Brazen with ten seconds to spare. We finish the run at 9.55 p.m. I give notes till 10.55 p.m. We just get a drink across the road and avoid going into another period of overtime. I drive home thinking even 65 per cent business won't be good enough (we've budgeted 55 per cent). What we need is a boffo metropolitan mega-hit, where we become one of the two of three hot shows in town and play to 95 per cent.*

---

*The Recruiting Officer* played to 59 per cent.

# Wednesday 20th July
### Final Dress Rehearsal

## Dear George,

A fretful day. Did some lighting with Chris Toulmin in the morning and got in a run of the second half in the afternoon. In the evening we did our first (and last) dress rehearsal. At this stage the acting always seems to have got knocked back a step or two by the technical demands and I want nothing more than to stop all this activity and refind the detail that has become mislaid. But I must wait. My notes in the afternoon are full of comments about offstage noise. Parallel to the action onstage is the action offstage, as dressers move into position to hijack exiting actors. Mark Omerod, the deputy stage manager, gets ready to do his moorhen and John Burgess the Deputy Master Carpenter, crosses the fly gallery getting ready to drop in the window-piece. All this movement should become minimized and orchestrated, and will in the end be as silent as a subterranean stream. At the moment it's more like a chattering brook. Peter suggests the actors discard their jackets for the midday scenes and immediately it begins to acquire a more summery feel. In the course of the morning, I adjust the flying speed of the incoming window so that it settles on its dead at the exact moment that Silvia meets Melinda in midstage (Act One, Scene Two). The scene changes are all a bit brutal. We haven't yet caught the flow of the play from one scene to the next. There are, of course, no blackouts, and the rhythm has to be maintained but the pace changed from scene to scene.

The Royal Court is still a hemp house, that is, it has an old-fashioned counterweighted flying system operated by flymen pulling on hemp ropes. The first flymen at Drury Lane were retired sailors from the Napoleonic Wars, experts at handling ropes. Nautical terms still survive, the stage floor is called the deck. But old-fashioned though this system may seem to me, it would have been revolutionary to you, for no theatre was purpose-built with a fly tower till after 1800. Your theatre was dependent on a system of shutters and tracked wing-pieces that gave perspective and depth. Gradually, through the eighteenth century, the forestage – with its doors straight on to the stage – was eliminated in order to increase capacity, and the actors were pushed further upstage into the scenery. Colley Cibber, your first Captain Brazen, thought this move retrogressive 'when the actors were in Possession of that forwarder space to advance upon, the Voice was then more in the Centre of the House . . . nor was the minutest Motion of a Feature . . . ever lost, as they frequently must be in the Obscurity of too great a Distance.' As the theatres grew in size, the dependence on scenic effects to retain audience interest grew. Conflagrations and aquatic effects become equally voguish in the last quarter of the eighteenth century, and the balance between text and scenery that has to be found afresh in every production became helplessly discordant. Garrick, who in his day was as famous an innovator as he was an actor, employed Philip de Loutherbourg as his designer (1772). His designs increasingly dominated the stage at Drury Lane and became the focus of critical debate. This reached a fitting climax in *Eidophysikon*, a production that took the ultimate step of dispensing altogether with script and actors, moving with measured grandeur from one scenic effect to the next. This spectaculist school of thought is not altogether dead today, and is perpetuated by the inclination to build epic arenas like the Olivier or the Sheffield Crucible. We then have to find simplistic dramas or snooker competitions to fill these grandiose spaces.

John Haynes came to the run this evening. He has been the house photographer at the Court since I started working there. I await his response. Apart from the people working on the show, all of whom now seem intimates after three days working together, John is always the first person to witness a play. He's not absolutely discreet, so word on the show will begin to ripple round London from tomorrow morning. Sometimes his ability to capture images you've hoped for, but not fully realized are there, is uncannily perceptive. He works swiftly and silently through the dress rehearsal, assessing a moment and pouncing. Afterwards he won't be drawn. He picked out Jim for particular approval. On the whole, it had been a worthy run, with the actors becoming more accurate but losing touch with the passion of the piece. We only have time for a brief notes session tonight, but I say I think they should re-contact the obsessions of their characters: Balance to preserve his estate, Silvia to capture Plume, Bullock to preserve Rose's reputation, Melinda to punish Worthy, and so on. The final scene which we worked on during the day is drawn together very well by David and finishes on an upbeat. There begins to be too much acting off the ball, with everybody working too hard in one of the play's very few group scenes, but otherwise, the teamwork and sense of each other has advanced since Saturday. I can see that the last twenty minutes (Act Five) needs to be played with great energy and purpose, or it will become anti-climactic. I can see the individual scenes that need work, and I can see where the play has improved, but I've rather lost sight of an overall picture. I can't any longer see the effect the play will have. Is it funny? Can one follow the plot? Will it be moving? Will it seem real? I plan to rehearse odd bits tomorrow afternoon, but not to run it through again. So, the first preview tomorrow night will also be our third run-through. Doubtless some of these questions will be answered then.

# Thursday 21st July
## First Preview

## Dear George,

Triumph.

It was a triumph last night. One of those exhilarating nights in the theatre that left me faint with pleasure and gratitude. I think there'll be times in the future when we perform your play much better, much more fluently and with rather more control, but it was thrilling for the actors, audience and me to discover your play and sense it coming to life. The triumph was yours: the wit and good nature of the play was evident and the story line clear. And, George, they laughed at your jokes! Brazen's mistaken apprehension that Balance's name is Laconic had the house chortling with merriment. The start, with Jude's drum heard distantly across the yard, coming closer and then thundering down the emergency exit was gripping and unexpected. Jim's recruiting speech however, which had been so powerful and charismatic in rehearsal, rather wobbled in the face of a fully lit and expectant audience. He said he lost his bottle because he saw Alison Steadman in the fourth row beaming at him encouragingly. The expository scenes between Kite and Plume, and then Worthy and Plume, were listened to attentively, and the wit of Plume's chat, long-buried under weeks of painstaking rehearsal, emerged sharply. The initial scene between Melinda and Silvia, which had caused Linda's eyebrows to meet with confused despair in rehearsal, was clearly characterised and beautifully controlled with the leadership of the scene changing hands decisively. Mark took charge as Balance and the audience warmed to Mossie, particularly a party of Chelsea pensioners brought in by the Press Office to mark the play's military connections. 'What a lovely pair of bristols' shouted one deaf old geezer whose hearing aid had been turned down. David only tripped over his clanking sword two or three times and Ron's Captain Brazen was much loved, getting a round on his first exit. I hadn't fully realized that the obtuseness of the word play and the obscurity of the jokes

178

wouldn't really put the audience off. They loved the character, and his snobbish obsessions were immediately accessible. The second act went well too: Jim's version of Kite's German doctor is hilarious and Lesley takes the lead in steering the play back to the main plot at the beginning of Act Five. The Court scene still needs more work and the end was confused with rather general enthusiastic playing, and David so determined to finish on an upbeat that he lost his lines completely and talked virtual nonsense.

But, really, George, a very good first performance. Above all, I was able to see the whole play clearly in a way I hadn't in the two previous run-throughs and now have a firm grasp of what work remains to be done. It looked good too: not so far off the Rowlandson cartoon that Peter and I had visualized all those weeks ago. The doubling seemed perfectly acceptable. Perhaps there's a moment of confusion when Silvia enters disguised as Wilful. Is she Silvia in disguise or is this another character? But a moment of doubt seems appropriate. The offstage life was vigorous too. Characters came on or went off in order to perform recognizable activities like buying drinks or selling chickens. Shrewsbury lives okay?

You will note that I've rather prematurely given the whole thing a good review. I was certainly relieved but I'm far from smug. Of course, the performances and the production will get better. The function of rehearsal is to map the extent and boundaries of the play while the ambition of performance is to colour and populate this territory. If the map is accurate then this becomes fruitful exploration for the actors whose performances will grow richer and denser. If, on the other hand, rehearsal hasn't defined the boundaries or has defined only a limited area, the actors' journey can wander all over the place. But whatever happens, from this point on, the director, unlike a conductor, begins to retreat from the central position he has filled in rehearsal and to become more of an animated and concerned bystander, whose occasional contribution becomes more detached and, hopefully, objective. From the moment of the first performance a production begins to set like jelly; it's still possible to give it one or two final transforming kicks but conditions begin to militate against this possibility. Every moment that is unstitched and re-examined for rehearsal during the day has to be bolted shut and made watertight for performance again that night. It can be done, but it's difficult. *Cloud Nine* had been two weeks on the road when Caryl and I totally revised the running order of the second half, and two weeks later we cut fifteen minutes from the whole play by nipping out a line here and half a speech there. Surgery of this kind is not required for *The Recruiting Officer*, but tomorrow we have some time to work. The call will be at 2.00 p.m. to work on the initial meeting between Plume and Silvia, which could be stiller and more electric. It's a short scene that didn't quite make its mark this evening. We only see Plume and Silvia together once but, as the whole plot springs from the intensity of their relationship, this meeting has to be more important. Melinda and Worthy at 3.00 p.m. Notes for the company at 4.00 p.m. and work the last scene if we get a chance before breaking at 6.00 p.m. Second preview at 8.00 p.m.

Not for the first time, I wondered this evening how close to you David Haig has become. He's revealed himself as an excellent leading man because, although he's a very deft actor, who feeds off direction, there's enough of this own charm and personality at the centre of the evening to command the audience's attention. He's boyish enough to engage in the romantic obsessions of Plume, but also man enough to renounce them with grace and a certain degree of enthusiasm. In the first scene, he discards his wig to wash at the pump after his long ride and reveals a receding hairline. Somehow I find the moment very human. It's the person beneath the hero that is so engaging. With Captain Plume but also with Lieutenant Farquhar. All the portraits that have come down to us show you in a full-bottomed wig with bony nose, attractive and quizzical eyes and a high forehead. But over the last eight weeks I feel I've caught you without your wig on. I know this to be a vulnerable position for an eighteenth-century gentleman. But it's been a real pleasure, George.

# EPILOGUE

I don't think I intended to end my correspondence with George after the first preview, but the next day I also began to re-engage with Timberlake and *Our Country's Good*. At this point, I think there was only the first half of a play that was to begin rehearsal ten days hence. We kept working on *The Recruiting Officer*, which improved through the previews although, for me, the most exciting moment would always remain the initial sense of it at that first preview. The production opened on Thursday 26 July 1988. The reviews were on the whole enthusiastic. Michael Billington wrote in the *Guardian*, 'Classics rarely surface at the Royal Court. But, when they do, a dead author is accorded the same respect as a living one. You feel that if George Farquhar could drop in on Max Stafford-Clark's excellent revival of *The Recruiting Officer*, he would actually recognise his own play.' The actors had absorbed the card exercises I used in rehearsal and rated the *Guardian* review a Red Nine. Some of the actors preferred not to read reviews. Linda Bassett was one. But she didn't mind being told 'Red Eight' in the *Sunday Times* or 'Black Four' in *Time Out*. Not everybody liked the production and some positively loathed it. Michael Coveney in the *Financial Times* gave it a Black Ten. He disliked the production so much he called for my head: 'Max Stafford-Clark, newly re-appointed as Artistic Director of the English Stage Company, has been in charge at the Royal Court for as long as Mrs Thatcher has been Prime Minister. My first and rather troubled reaction to his revival of George Farquhar's Restoration masterpiece is that the length of tenure is beginning to close down his artistic vision . . . The major mistake is to treat it like a Caryl Churchill play, actors doubling so many roles that each one is deprived of its own true life and flavour . . . the production . . . is as dull as it is misguided.' Michael was the only critic to re-review Bill Gaskill's production of 1963 rather than engage with our work. But then he would, wouldn't he? Coveney is certainly a peppery fellow, but he's also a conscientious romantic whose views of theatre have been shaped by great past productions that, over the passage of years, have become elevated to the status of icons. *The Recruiting Officer* was one of them. He tries hard to like my work, and indeed sometimes succeeds, but his impatience usually prevails. By inclination, he prefers to write about great actors biting off huge, chunky roles. And he writes well of them. It's ironic, though, that the critic of the *Financial Times* should find the economic reasons that made the doubling obligatory so incomprehensible.

On Monday, August 1st, we started work on *Our Country's Good*. The read-through was the first time the actors had had sight of the play and they responded positively. The structure was sound and remained very largely the same over the next five weeks. Late in rehearsal, Timberlake added a scene between Mary Brenham and John Wisehammer, and we re-structured the running order at the beginning of the second half. The actors had become a powerful and unified ensemble through our work together on *The Recruiting Officer*, and their confidence made for a third voice in the debate that occupied the initial rehearsals.

One early conflict with Timberlake was over the first scene. This was a collage of antiphonal interior monologues from the convicts in the hold of the transport. Individually, they contained fine writing but it established a poetic reality that the play then discarded. Another key decision concerned the scene Timberlake had called 'The Authorities Discuss the Merits of the Theatre'. This was the scene where the Officers' Mess discussed the desirability of the impending production. It seemed important to have a full Officers' Mess so that as wide a range of opinions as possible could be aired. It could be done with the six male actors, or we could have a full house of the whole company. This was attractive but would involve the four women taking men's roles. Not all the reviews of *The Recruiting Officer* had approved of Linda Bassett playing Thomas Appletree and the company were understandably tentative. Inevitably, it would establish a certain kind of theatricality which would determine the style of the production. I wasn't certain but on the whole Timberlake and I favoured the bolder option. A third controversy concerned a dream scene towards the end of the first half. Ralph Clark's extraordinary tortured dreams fill the first volume of his journal and Keneally had drawn on them imaginatively in the novel. Timberlake had written a dream sequence in which Ralph's wife, Alicia, appeared to be cavorting with Robert Sideway, the convict acting enthusiast. I resisted the scene at length, probably unreasonably: I don't fancy dream scenes and have no original idea of how to set about staging them. It would also have involved Mossie appearing as yet one more character for a single scene.

Phoning Timberlake at any moment when she wasn't in rehearsal replaced writing to George, but Philip Howard, the assistant director, kept a journal. It was his first involvement with a production of this kind and he records the vigorous but fractious nature of early rehearsals with ill-concealed alarm:

> Tuesday August 2nd: Max asks Timberlake to justify scene 10 ('Ralph Dreams of His Beloved Wife') – he's made no secret of disliking it!
>
> After tea: Max thinks we've done enough going through the play; time to do some rehearsing, so he picks on what is rapidly becoming the old chestnut of Act 1, Scene 10. Max's motive appears to be to show that it's unstageable – but how can you put on a scene without wanting to do it? Alicia is to be alarming, maternal and sexy. Max corners Timberlake into giving the scene *one* main function. Answer is to show Ralph as a disturbed young man. We rehearse the scene, Max wonders whether the function couldn't be carried out more dramatically by a monologue. David (Haig) reads out one of Clark's monologues from latter's *Journals*. Well, it has to be said, Timberlake says that when she hears a monologue from a diary she tunes out. Max says same thing about dreams on stage. This isn't going well – everyone is talking and giving opinions (especially Nick Dunning). Everyone knows that Max isn't happy – perhaps it would be better if he were *more* authoritative and just cut it now. Trouble is, he feels so much pressure with this project anyway, he doesn't want to do anything so cavalier.

This is a kindly rationalisation on Philip's part. However, he is inclined to mistake healthy scepticism for dislike, or a degree of wary silence on the part of the actors for unanimous approval. In fact, our efforts to stage the dream scene had almost persuaded me of its possibilities. Nor should a director be too authoritarian, particularly in the early days of rehearsal. If you proceed by argument and debate it's important to know which arguments to lose as well as which ones to win. When we had worked through the play and arrived at the dream scene some weeks later, its purpose seemed accomplished elsewhere and it was quietly dropped without much further discussion.

Philip Howard's journal records an early debate on 'The Authorities Discuss the Merits of the Theatre'.

> Mark (Lambert) feels that Major Ross' personal status is too low. He and Captain Campbell (Jim Broadbent) are too jokey. But his status among other officers was a paradox: a major and yet a laughing-stock because so extremist. Max says Ross *is* written as a comic role in this scene but that doesn't mean he can't take tragic weight elsewhere. Mark thinks the scene is too long and so does David. Max won't let them cut it till we've been through it again.

Part of the actors' resistance to the scene was their lack of excitement at what seemed a dry, intellectual discussion. Timberlake pointed out that debate would have been a major excitement to a group of eighteenth-century gentlemen. Timberlake, who would have been at home in Madame de Staël's salon, has a pellucid intelligence which never let us down. Part of the difficulty of the scene was that Timberlake was trying to write three characters of equal intellectual stature; Watkin Tench, the conservative, Davy Collins, the cynic, and Governor Phillip, the radical humanitarian. I recalled Wally Shawn saying that it was impossible for a writer to create a character more intelligent than himself. And very nearly impossible to write a character as intelligent who held views to which the writer was antagonistic. Through the five weeks rehearsal we returned to 'Authorities Discuss . . .' again and again; cutting and honing it. It set the intellectual premise from which the emotion in the play would spring in the second half. Governor Phillip believed that the most loathsome, foul-mouthed convict had the possibility of redemption. He was as passionate in his conviction as Major Ross was in his. The scene was the mainspring of the first half. Philip Howard wrote in his journal (August 8th):

> Methuen will have to wait for re-writes – if we only have 3+ weeks to get this show on the road they can wait to print the playtext. Whole morning spent in hot-off-the-press re-write of 'Authorities Discuss . . .' Changes dictated, actions clarified, moves worked out. David is frightened of Clark being depicted as too weak. He shouldn't always equate

theatrical viability with aggression. In fact, he's not really being humble enough in front of largely antagonistic superior officers.

This was quite true. In the hierarchy of the officers' mess, Clark was insignificant. But as director of the play he was a central figure in the audience's perception. Also, in this particular scene, he surprises his brother officers with unexpected eloquence. This set up a fascinating and complex scene but inevitably it involved more changes. Philip Howard (17th August): '7.45 pm. Max has received proofs of Act 1, scenes 1–6, from Methuen – all wrong of course, but it's no use getting in a panic about it because this is going to go on and on and on and on. As usual, Max just doesn't understand how much time has been spent upstairs trying to get this right.' Governor Phillip teaches the Officers' Mess in this scene by the Socratic Method. I compare him, ironically, to a Joint Stock director: superficial encouragement of democracy, followed by autocratic final decision-taking. It was not a comparison that went unnoticed.

The first scene changed shape continually through rehearsal and didn't arrive at its final form till the second preview. Philip Howard's journal records our attempts to wrestle it to the ground:

Wednesday 3rd August: afternoon. Timberlake brought along re-writes of the first two scenes, in effect just drastically cut versions of old ones. Max comments that these monologues shouldn't be introverted; there must be a *reason* for saying all this. A thorough going-over of Scene 1 with hundreds of changes. Oh dear. Next, an ORGY, recreating the tableaux where, for the first time, we try heaving sheet over the company with them crawling out from underneath – as they land on the beach – 'rutting'.

The night after the convicts had been finally landed in Sydney Cove, there was an extraordinary and terrifying orgy in the middle of a ferocious storm with the rum-maddened sailors slithering through the mud in pursuit of the women convicts. In the middle of this a sheep was struck dead by lightning. The vivid description in Robert Hughes' *The Fatal Shore* is compelling: but our attempts to bring this event to the stage were doomed. With Joint Stock in the seventies it would have been fine, but in the eighties, actors just won't take orgies seriously.

Philip records the moment when at last we began to find the structure for the first scene.

Saturday 13th August. 4.20 pm. Attempt to sort out that old chestnut, the first scene of the play – whole company are now either going to be beaten or do the beating, except Ralph who is to count the number of lashes. Max splits up Jim's hunger speech between all of them. A chorus of starved ranting. Next we practise flagellation. Mark, Nick and I disappear in Stalls Bar for a warm-up. They both complain that this is like Drama School, which isn't giving Max much of a chance. What is then worked out is a sequence from start of play into Scene 3, and it is *good*: first the sound of slow, calculated, counted lashes, which are then overlapped by the 'hunger' and 'cunt' speeches. Victim faints, is cut down and, as he is brought downstage, lights will go up on the huddle of other prisoners, who split to avoid him. Linda announces Scene 2 title, and Jude, on high, does the few lines of 'A Lone Aboriginal Australian', and straight into Scene 3, 'Punishment', a scene in which Governor Phillip leads a discussion on the first hangings. Very speedy costume changes are necessary. But unlike previous occasions Max is very anti anyone pondering over theatrical difficulties. We run it twice and it is *good*. Dare I send this to Methuen now?

The answer was: not quite. The scene went through further changes, and John Arscott's speech about hunger was not cut till after the first preview. But I learned to love the first scene. In performance, it was one of the scenes I enjoyed watching most. It had a filmic quality, with the images emerging slowly from the mist. David's red-coated officer, bewigged, erect, still, counting the lashes; Nick stripped to the waist, strapped to the triangle motionless. And the huddle of convicts downstage like a Doré print. Mark, with the cat, emerged from the wings moving like a fast bowler, the delivery point Robert Sideway's (Nick's) back. The scene pulled us into the eighteenth century and set brutality firmly on the agenda for the evening.

Meanwhile, the actors were still performing *The Recruiting Officer* four times a week. Their concentration began to drift round 4.00 pm every afternoon as they preserved their energy for the evening performance. Philip Howard's journal, Saturday 13th August: 'Punishingly hot afternoon. The actors found performing last night very stifling. So now the air conditioning is going to be switched on at select intervals.'

Frayed with fatigue, always aware that we were fighting against the time factor, we kept at it, but something had to give. Philip wrote:

Monday 15th August. These days of rehearsal are different to those of *The Recruiting Officer* – a constant tension, which *never* seems to be released. We do not relax – everything is a rush. How spoilt we were with *TRO*. Today Max decided to postpone the opening of *OCG* by four days. Administrative side of building are furious that they weren't consulted about this. Attempting to co-ordinate re-writes for Methuen is very difficult – they haven't received any of Act Two yet. Whole afternoon in the photocopying room.

Poor Philip. I sense the peace of the photocopying room become a haven away from the heat and oppression of rehearsal. But I think there were moments when we all panicked. On the 16th August I wrote: 'I can't even stage things. Set appears to have no focus. I think we're sliding towards a disaster. I can't see my way through it at all. Even with the postponement there just isn't enough time. Feel knackered. Two plays back to back is a killer.'

But I have to say that this despair is customary. It's lucky that we have such limited ability to retain the memory of physical and mental exhaustion or I would never direct again. Timberlake would write in the morning and come in after lunch. We would show her the scene we had worked on that day, then read through the new scene. There was no production in the Theatre Upstairs at the time and this became our rehearsal room. On the wall, we chalked a chronology of the scenes in the play from January 26th, 1788, the day the First Fleet landed to June 4th, 1789, the date of the convict performance. Every scene was given a specific date. I can't remember the moment when it all began to seem possible rather than impossible but gradually Philip Howard began to spend more time in rehearsal than he did in the photocopying room. I've emphasised the scenes that were the hardest to crack, but there were also ones that slotted sweetly into place, like 'The First Rehearsal' or 'A Love Scene'. Some of Timberlake's finest writing emerged in this period. And then there were scenes that we chipped away at, making gradual progress each time we rehearsed, consolidating the through-line of the characters and clarifying the scenes.

One evening, at about 9.30 pm, we made a break-through

with the penultimate scene, 'A Question of Liz'. The foul-mouthed and brutalised Liz Morden (Linda Bassett) had been condemned to hang for stealing food. She's probably innocent, but sticks to her convict vow of silence and stubbornly declines to clear herself. Collins, the colony's Advocate General, is concerned that the law will be discredited if there's a miscarriage of justice. He and Governor Phillip are also reluctant to hang a woman. It had taken the latter part of the afternoon and all of the evening to sift through the different lines of argument, and to clarify the objectives and powers of this tribunal. Was Collins seeking a re-trial? If Phillip had a power of veto why was it necessary for Liz to speak? As we became tired it became natural to hit the stale and irritable tones of people who had been arguing for four hours and were at an impasse. Linda had no lines till the end of the scene and we had rehearsed since tea without reaching this point. Each time we neared it something else would go awry. We would work it out and go back. When we broke again, Linda moved away and sat by herself. I realised she hadn't spoken for over three hours. After the break, I ran the scene. When we reached the point where Linda spoke, the moment was electric. Our own anticipation and anxiety parallelled the characters in the play. In the final lines of the scene Ron Cook as the Governor says, 'Liz I hope you are good in your part.' Timberlake has Linda respond, 'Your excellency I will endeavour to speak Mr Farquhar's lines with the elegance and clarity their own worth commands.'

It was a thrilling fusion of heart and intellect. The thesis behind the play was illuminated with enormous emotional power. It was equally thrilling to reflect, as I drove home, that there remained only one more scene to broach. This was 'Backstage' the final scene of the play where the convict actors are preparing for their performance. The scenes of debate in the play are alternated with scenes of rehearsal. It was really a Royal Court work scene where the rhythms of a very ordinary activity reveal a secret world. There were moments when the whole group focused on one moment together, as when Ron Cook as Wisehammer recites his prologue from which Timberlake had taken the play's title. Other moments showed backstage activity as actors went over lines, made each other up and got into their costumes. This was one scene the actors didn't need to research. I enjoyed bringing first one moment and then another into focus. We looked at Hogarth's 'Strolling Actors Dressing in a Barn' and some of the grouping in our scene was based on that wonderfully evocative picture. Since there was no problem in clearing the stage for another scene we were able to accumulate an evocative pile of props and costumes during the course of the scene. Midway through the afternoon, I caught Neil O'Malley's eye. He was supposed to be on the book (prompting) but I could see that he was fascinated and visibly moved by the eighteenth-century recreation of the backstage life so familiar to him. In the course of the afternoon, Jenny Cook, the wardrobe mistress, came by to drop off some costumes. She stayed too. And by the end of the afternoon, I had come to see how moving Timberlake's final scene would be. We had learned from our evening at Wormwood Scrubs and there was no apology for the passion and commitment with which the actors prepared for their performance. David Haig, as Ralph Clark the director, was trembling with excitement and emotion as he made Ralph's final speech thanking his actors and acknowledging the experience they had been through together. In the hushed pause that follows, Lesley Sharp as Mary Brenham whispers, 'I love this'. Her journey from cowed and brutalised convict to Australia's first leading lady was complete.

The public response and the critical reception of *Our Country's Good*, by no means always the same thing, was universally favourable. It wasn't a huge hit to begin with but through September and October houses built steadily and the final weeks played to packed houses. Not the least of the play's achievements was the resonant chord it touched in London's beleaguered theatrical community. A play that proclaimed the power and enduring worth of theatre, and that celebrated its centrality to our lives, was of importance in the third term of a government who deemed subsidy a dirty word. Dr Success transformed our exhausting rehearsal experience into a shared Amazonian adventure that we had had together. We all felt very close. Timberlake's first-night card to me, said simply, 'I cherish every argument.'